Contents

KV-578-045

Editor's note and bibliography

Chaucer is our greatest comic poet, and *The Canterbury Tales* is his masterpiece. Yet Chaucer's poetry is not a subject for general reading, but of specialist study. The reason for this is that his language is not easy for the general reader to read and understand. The English language of the fourteenth century was different from the language we speak today, and some trouble must be taken in learning these differences before a proper understanding of the meaning can be gained. And further, when one has learned to read Chaucer and to understand the meaning, some knowledge is necessary of the age in which he lived, and his place in it, before the work of this colourful and humorous poet can be fully appreciated and enjoyed.

These notes are aimed primarily at students coming fresh to Chaucer in their studies of English literature. An attempt has been made to set out, as briefly and simply as possible, the areas of knowledge which are necessary for the proper understanding and appreciation of a selected text in the context of examination requirements at Ordinary and Advanced Levels. It is hoped, however, that the notes have been prepared in such a way that the student will enjoy the task of understanding and appreciating this wonderful poetry with its melodic style, gentle satire and rollicking humour, and even to acquire a taste for Chaucer which will lead to wider reading and a deeper appreciation of his work.

The Editor wishes to acknowledge his indebtedness to the various works he has studied, and particularly to the editions of Chaucer's works by Professors W. W. Skeat and F. N. Robinson (it is on the latter's work that the text of this edition is based – *The Complete Works of Geoffrey Chaucer*, 2nd ed., 1957, with revised punctuation and spelling by James Winny. CUP,

I. G. Handyside MA

Brodie's Notes on Chaucer's

The Miller's Tale

MACMILLAN

First published 1978 by Pan Books Ltd

Reprinted 1992 by
THE MACMILLAN PRESS LTD
Houndmills, Basingstoke, Hampshire RG21 2XS
and London
Companies and representatives
throughout the world

ISBN 0–333–58064–8

Printed in Great Britain by
Clays Ltd, St Ives plc, Bungay, Suffolk

1971); and the editions of several of Chaucer's *Tales* edited by F. W. Robinson and published by James Brodie Ltd.

Bibliography

For those who wish to carry their study of Chaucer beyond what is possible to include in a small volume of notes, a selection of books that may be helpful is listed below:

The Poet Chaucer, Nevill Coghill, OUP Paperbacks

An Introduction to Chaucer, Hussey, Spearing and Winny, CUP

English Social History, Trevelyan (Chaps 1 and 2) Longmans, also Penguin

Chaucer's World, ed. M. Hussey, CUP

Pelican Guide to English Literature, Vol. 1, The Age of Chaucer, Penguin

It is recommended that students should read a selection of the tales from the translation into modern verse by Nevill Coghill – *The Canterbury Tales*, translated by Nevill Coghill, Penguin Classics.

It is also recommended that students should listen to a recording of Chaucer read with the original pronunciation – *The Prologue to The Canterbury Tales*, read in Middle English by Nevill Coghill, Norman Davis and John Burrow, Argo Record Company, London, No. PLP 1001 (LP).

A brief description of
Chaucer's life and works

Geoffrey Chaucer was born about 1340 near the Tower of London. He was born into the age of Edward III, and of the Black Prince, into the Age of Chivalry and the magnificent court of Edward III with knights and ladies, heraldry and tournaments, minstrels and poetry, music and story-telling.

Chaucer entered into this rich and colourful courtly world at an early age, when he became a page in the household of the Countess of Ulster, wife to Lionel, later Duke of Clarence, and one of the sons of Edward III. This was clearly arranged by his parents, who had some contacts at Court. His mother's first husband had been Keeper of the King's Wardrobe, and there can be little doubt that she had something to do with the appointment of Chaucer's father as deputy to the King's Butler. The first record of Geoffrey Chaucer appears in an account book, dating from 1357, which records a payment by the royal household to a London tailor for a cloak, multi-coloured breeches and a pair of shoes for the young page Chaucer. It was in the Duke's great houses in London and Yorkshire that the young page would have learned the elegant and aristocratic code of manners, and made the acquaintance of the high and the noble. He would have learned French and Latin, the language of the Court, the Church and the educated classes. It was also one of the duties of a page to play and sing, and to recite poetry.

The next record we have is that Chaucer was taken prisoner by the French in 1359, during one of the campaigns in The Hundred Years' War, and ransomed in the following year – the King himself contributing £16 (a very large sum in those days) of the money. So Chaucer must have seen active service in the French wars, probably as a squire attending on one of the nobles, like the squire in the *Canterbury Tales* who attended on the Knight, his father. For the upper classes, the experience of being a prisoner of war in the Age of Chivalry was not too uncomfortable. It was normal for the 'prisoner' to be entertained as a 'house guest' until the ransom was paid, and it is probable that during this enforced stay in France Chaucer became thoroughly versed in French literature, particularly the *Roman de la Rose* (the procedure manual, as it were, for 'courtly love'), which was to have such an important influence on his literary work.

After his ransom was paid, Chaucer returned to his Court duties, and was soon in a more elevated position. He became one of the valets in attendance on the King. In 1366 his father died and his mother married again. It is probable that in the same year he married Philippa, daughter of Sir Payne Roet and sister of Katherine Swynford, the mistress and later third wife to John of Gaunt. Philippa was a lady-in-waiting to the Queen. As a valet to the King, Chaucer would carry candles 'before the King', tidy up his bedroom and attend to a variety of duties which were to become more and more concerned with affairs of state. In 1386 he was sent abroad on the official business of the Crown. About this time he was promoted from valet to palace official. It appears that Chaucer went soldiering again in 1369, probably on one of John of Gaunt's campaigns in Picardy. In 1370 he was abroad again on the King's service, and we can now see him becoming a trusted civil servant as he was frequently sent on missions to France, Flanders and Italy. During his visits to Italy on official business Chaucer took the opportunity to become familiar with Italian literature, most especially the works of Petrarch, Boccaccio and Dante, which were to influence much of his subsequent poetry.

In 1374 he was promoted to a senior position as Comptroller of Customs and Subsidy (for wool, skins and hides) at the Port of London, and the City of London bestowed on him the lease of a house in Aldgate.

From about 1380 Chaucer settled down to his life as senior

customs official, as there is only one record of further journeys abroad. He must have been respected as a man of affairs, as he became a Justice of the Peace in 1385, and a Member of Parliament, or Knight of the Shire for Kent, soon afterwards.

It was during these years that Chaucer found time to write seriously. His early literary attempts were influenced considerably by French literature. Then, when John of Gaunt left the country in 1386 on an adventure to claim the crown of Castile, the King's uncle, the Duke of Gloucester, took charge of the country's affairs (Richard being not yet of age), and Chaucer suffered from the new influences in royal patronage. He lost his Comptrollership of Customs, he was not re-elected to Parliament and he had to give up his house in Aldgate. We even learn that he felt himself in danger of being sued for debt. Chaucer had now plenty of time to ponder and at this time he must have been preparing *The Canterbury Tales*.

In 1389 a rumour was abroad that the great Duke of Lancaster (Chaucer's patron John of Gaunt) was returning home. This helped the young King Richard II in taking over the reins of power from his uncle Gloucester. It has been stated that the young King Richard knew Chaucer and liked his poetry. There must be some substance in this, as shortly afterwards Chaucer was appointed Clerk of the King's Works. John of Gaunt returned to England in November 1389, and for the rest of his life Chaucer was to enjoy royal patronage and a comfortable living. It was in these years of semi-retirement that *The Canterbury Tales* were written. Alas, Chaucer died without having finished his masterpiece. His tomb in Westminster Abbey gives the date of his death – October 1400.

It seems probable that 1387 was the approximate date of commencement for *The Canterbury Tales*. Chaucer's renown rests mainly on his work, but in terms of volume the *Tales* form less than half of his writing which has come down to us. Besides a number of shorter poems, there are five other major works in verse and two or three in prose. Chaucer's most important production during his first tentative years as a writer was his translation he probably made of the *Roman de la Rose*, the style and content of which was to have such a great influence on his writing. His first major poem was *The Book of the Duchess*, a poem steeped in the French tradition, written about 1370 to commemorate the death of Blanche, Duchess of Lancaster, and wife of his patron, John of Gaunt. This was the first of four love-vision poems, the others being *The House of Fame*, *The Parliament of Fowls* and *The Legend of Good Women* (whose date is doubtful). Chaucer's works can be conveniently grouped into three parts, the French period, the Italian period and the English period; and, generally speaking, the periods follow one another in chronological sequence. The French period showed influence of the *Roman de la Rose*, and included the love-vision poems. The Italian period (1380–5) is marked by the narrative poem *Troilus and Criseyde*, which rehandles a theme of the Italian poet Boccaccio. *Troilus and Criseyde* is a masterpiece, and is still considered to be the finest narrative poem in English, full of beauty and lyrical quality, and delightful humour in the character of Pandarus. The English period (1389-1400) is the last, and is the period when Chaucer reached his full maturity as a dramatic poet. This is the period of *The Canterbury Tales*, a collection of tales and tellers which is unique in English literature. Chaucer died before he could complete this great masterpiece.

It must be emphasized that these terms, 'French', 'Italian', 'English' for Chaucer's literary life only indicate predominant influences: the stories in *The Canterbury Tales* are drawn from far and wide; *The Knight's Tale*, for instance, again owes its theme to a story by Boccaccio.

The setting of the *Tale*

The Miller's Tale is but one of a collection of stories which make up *The Canterbury Tales*, his most ambitious and comprehensive work, and his last. Some of the tales may have been composed during earlier periods of Chaucer's literary career and brought together, with others specially written for the purpose, as a collection of stories told within the framework of a pilgrimage to Canterbury. There are many examples in the literature of the Middle Ages of collections of stories, and there is no doubt that Chaucer was familiar with some of them. Most of Chaucer's stories did not originate with him, any more than Shakespeare originated his own plots; nevertheless, *The Canterbury Tales* are unique. By choosing a pilgrimage as the frame-story within which to tell his tales, Chaucer, in a brilliant stroke of genius, was able to bring together as pilgrims a representative group of many of the various classes of English society of his time, and to allocate to each pilgrim a tale suited to character and status.

Chaucer's ambitious plan for *The Canterbury Tales* was never completed. In the *Prologue* we are told that each pilgrim will tell four tales, two on the outward and another two on the homeward journey. But the company never reaches Canterbury and there are manuscripts of tales for only twenty-three of the thirty pilgrims, and these incompletely arranged, and in some cases unfinished. Nevertheless, this partly completed work is the masterpiece of comic poetry in English literature.

The dramatic coherence of *The Canterbury Tales* is fashioned by the *Prologue*, which sets the scene of the pilgrimage to Canterbury, and introduces the pilgrims by a striking series of word portraits. The portraits of the pilgrims leap out of the pages with all the vividness of description and character of great portrait-painting, and with astounding originality and realism. As Nevill Coghill comments, 'The result was a new sort of poetical truth, the creation of a poetry of fact by a wise, sure-eyed and sensitive selection of daily detail, mellowed and harmonized by a humane and often an amused approval, qualified wherever approval was withdrawn by an ironical wit. It was a new way of looking at people.' So diverse are the characters, and so vivid the portraiture, that the *Prologue* has been described as the National Portrait Gallery of medieval England; the portraits of a nation, of 'high and low, old and young, male and female, lay and clerical, learned and ignorant, rogue and righteous, land and sea, town and country.' The portrait of the Miller from the *Prologue* to *The Canterbury Tales* is included before the text of the *Miller's Tale*. He is described as a big, burly fellow, strong as an ox; with a broad red beard and a wart on the very tip of his nose. In character he is a loud-mouthed, vulgar rogue who delighted in telling dirty stories.

The portrait and character of the Miller is included because it is an essential part of the *Prologue* to the *Miller's Tale*, and the tale itself. In keeping with the diversity of characters is the wide range of stories which are assigned to the pilgrims, each tale being suited to the character and vocation of the teller. Almost every type of medieval fiction is represented – the romance of chivalry, the courtly lay, the beast-epic, the legend or saint's life, the sermon, and the coarse realistic 'fabliau'; and it is this last, the 'fabliau', that is represented by the *Miller's Tale*. In the *Prologue* to the *Miller's Tale* Chaucer mentions the other types of stories offered in the selection in an attempt to excuse the inclusion of such a vulgar and scurrilous story, such 'harlotrie', as the Miller's:

And therfore, whoso list it nat yheere,
Turne over the leef and chese another tale; ...
Of storial thing that toucheth gentillesse
And eek moralitee and hoolynesse.

In the *Prologue* to *The Canterbury Tales* we learn that Chaucer had already taken up his quarters at the Tabard Inn, Southwark in preparation for his pilgrimage the next day to Canterbury, when some twenty-nine other people arrive at the inn for the same purpose. The landlord of the Tabard Inn, the host, Harry Bailly, learning the purpose of the assembled company, proposed that the pilgrims should entertain themselves during the journey by telling one another stories. The company accepted this suggestion, and when the Host announced his intention to join the party on the pilgrimage, decided to appoint him as organizer and judge of the tales. There would be a prize for the best tale told, which would be a good supper at the Tabard Inn at the expense of the other companions. Certain matters of discipline were also discussed, and all the company agreed to abide by the rules laid down by the Host, any breach of which would involve a fine amounting to the travelling expenses of the whole company. The company started off on the journey to Canterbury early the next morning. It was decided by lot that the Knight, the most distinguished member of the party, should tell the first tale.

The Knight, very properly and entirely according to character, tells a tale of chivalric romance, abounding in the artificial manners of courtly love, of descriptions of temples and gardens, of battle and of nobility and philosophy. The Knight's tale is greatly applauded by the company, and the Host is very pleased by the successful start to his arrangements.

The end of the *Knight's Tale* is followed by the *Prologue* to the *Miller's Tale*. This *Prologue* is the link joining the two tales, and serves as comment on the tale just told, and as an introduction to the next. The *Prologues*, or links, also act as dramatic interludes between the tales, adding drama and giving movement and reality to the frame-story.

In the *Prologue* to the *Miller's Tale*, the Host invites the Monk to take the next turn at story-telling, with the intention of determining an orderly sequence of story-telling by social precedence, when he is rudely interrupted by the Miller, who is drunk and insists on telling the next story, which is to be a 'noble tale' that he knows which will match that of the Knight. For the sake of peace the Host has no alternative but to accept. The Miller then enlarges on this 'noble tale' that he is about to tell, it being a tale after the fashion of a 'saintly biography' – about the cuckolding of a carpenter! This is a taunt at the Reeve, who was by trade a carpenter, and not surprisingly stimulates an angry exchange between these two choleric characters. The Reeve replies to the Miller's taunting tale by telling the third tale, a similar scurrilous story about the cuckolding of a Miller. Thus the random order of story-telling is established by dramatic incident and without regard for social precedence.

The origin of the *Tale*

The Miller's Tale belongs to a type of narrative widely current in medieval Europe, and known as the 'fabliaux'. A 'fabliau' was a short story for and about the lower social classes. The main characteristics were coarseness, humour and realism; with the narrative turning on plot and intrigue. *The Miller's Tale* retains essentially the same characteristics – it is plain-spoken, comic and indecent, and the fast-moving narrative concerns a plot against a 'sely carpenter'.

The researches of Chaucerian scholars have unearthed several versions of European tales similar to *The Miller's Tale*. Some of the stories, mainly German and Flemish, include the same ingredients, particularly the farce of one man in a tub suspended from the ceiling while another takes a woman to bed, the atmosphere of impending disaster from flood, the arrival of a third man leading to the 'misdirected kiss', the application of a red-hot instrument and the subsequent confusion and ridicule.

The theme of *The Miller's Tale* is that of a 'fabliau', but Chaucer's treatment transforms the story of the 'misdirected kiss' into a masterpiece of comic narrative – indeed, to what has been called 'the best comic story in the world'. To the clumsiness and lack of gaiety of the original, Chaucer introduces design and structure, a brilliance of description and characterization, wit and humour, and all in clear, sharp, incomparable comic poetry.

The plot

The plot is a supreme example of structural design, the sort of design we look for in the best detective stories, where the story has a beginning, middle and end; where action, dialogue and character are interwoven with absolute relevance; and where there are clues in abundance, and no loose ends lying about at the end.

The story of *The Miller's Tale* is ingenious. Throughout the plot each new development is carefully prepared in advance, with background, character and action fused in a complex but perfectly designed structure which leads naturally to the final dénouement.

The plot is foreshadowed in the *Prologue* to the tale. We know from the *General Prologue* that the Miller is a loud-mouthed, vulgar lout who delights in telling dirty stories. In his rude interruption of the Host and his argument with the Reeve, the drunken Miller gives out some clues about the subject matter of his 'noble tale' – the cuckolding of husbands, the unfaithfulness of wives and the stupidity of inquiring too closely into either the misbehaviour of wives or the mysteries of God. Chaucer, as narrator, rounds this off by making excuses for including in his collection a tale of such vulgarity. The audience (or in our case the reader) has now a pretty good idea of what's coming – certainly the opposite of 'noble', and full of *lewed dronken harlotrie*. The feeling of anticipation is already on us.

The plot of the tale itself starts right from the first line with the introduction of the characters, the 'dramatis personae' – the student Nicholas, the rich old carpenter, his beautiful young wife Alison, and the foppish parish clerk Absolon – and sets the scene with the love-affair of the student and the wife, and their decision to plan a night together.

The distinguishing characteristic of Chaucer's plot structure and poetry is that every line, almost every word, is full of meaning and adds to the setting of the scene or to the development of the plot. The portraits of the characters themselves point to their subsequent behaviour and presage the end result – the good-looking and educated Nicholas, very experienced with girls, with a determined and clever mind much occupied with the complex science of astrology and therefore able to make forecasts; the rich, mean, jealous and ignorant old carpenter, over-possessive of his beautiful wife and who, consequently, is in for trouble; the young wife, beautiful, decorative, sensual and unsatisfied. It is clear at this stage of the plot that Nicholas and Alison are made for each other, and that the stupid old carpenter will rightly be deceived by the clever sly young student. Chaucer then adds a brilliant touch by introducing an additional element into the plot in the character of Absolon, the parish clerk, whose complex portrait points dramatically to his subsequent behaviour and ruin – the fastidious, over-dressed, effeminate young man who thinks that he is in love with Alison.

This is the 'beginning' of the story – the characters are introduced and the scene is set. In terms of plot, everything has been subtly prepared, and precisely placed in the overall structure. In fact, the scene and the clues are neatly summarized for us, initially at the end of each character portrait – the comfortable and idle position of Nicholas (ll.111–12), the problems of a rich old carpenter with a beautiful young wife (ll. 123–4), the sexual attractiveness of the beautiful young wife (ll. 161–2) and the fastidious over-sensitivity of the parish clerk Absolon (ll.229–30) – and finally, at the end of the 'beginning', thus projecting the next or 'middle', phase of the plot (ll.289–90). The first part is full of descriptive poetry of rare quality, with bursts of dramatic poetry in the most free and natural style when the action demands – for the arguments between the Host and the Miller, and the Miller and the Reeve; and for the love affair of Nicholas and Alison.

From now on the action quickens and the poetry reflects the change in tempo and the developing drama.

The 'middle' of the story consists of the preparation and the execution of the plan by Nicholas to deceive the carpenter. This is an ingeniously contrived plan with precise timing based on the pretended astrological forecast of another great flood. The previous references to astrology are developed step by step to impress the ignorant and gullible old carpenter. First by creating the right atmosphere – Nicholas' feigned madness and the understandable fear and panic of the carpenter; secondly by introducing the subject of the flood – the results of astrologic forecasts and God's mysterious purpose, thus 'brain-washing' the old carpenter by technical jargon and the fear of God, and playing on his pathetic determination to save his adored wife from drowning; and thirdly, the details of the plan to escape the flood. The middle part ends with the execution of the plan and the satisfaction of the lovers.

The last part of the plot, the 'end', covers the consequences of all the previous actions and patterns of behaviour in a brilliant, fast-moving, richly comic sequence of events, narrated at an ever-increasing pace in a natural and comic dramatic verse, with all the earlier clues and hints of poetic justice developed to their logical conclusion, and the whole story tied up and summarized in the last five lines.

The construction, the descriptive power, the humour and the narrative style of poetry of Chaucer's tales are unique in medieval story-telling. In *The Miller's Tale* the carefully constructed fabric of the fantastic plot is interwoven with threads of realism in the imagery of daily life, the factual style of conversation and 'real' characters; and all in the spirit of gaiety, vitality, gentle satire and rollicking humour. Nevill Coghill has summarized Chaucer's style in a sentence, 'The quality of this new poetry can be tasted in a single line, perhaps the funniest line in the funniest story in the world: "Tehee!" quod she, and clapte the window to.'

The characters

Chaucer's work is renowned for brilliant and extended portraiture, matching vivid description with subtle characterization, and combining utmost economy with touches of bright detail. His genius for painting-with-words is nowhere more evident than in *The Miller's Tale*. The portrait of Alison is amongst the most vivid and beautiful in English literature; and that of Absolon amongst the most complex and subtle in short-story writing.

The portrayal of character in *The Miller's Tale* is not just an exercise of poetic craftsmanship on its own, but an integral part of the plot as a whole, as has been explained in the previous section. Nevertheless, it is a revealing exercise to stand some way back from the tale and examine the supreme quality of Chaucer's powers of characterization.

There are five characters in *The Miller's Tale* – the carpenter, his wife Alison, the student Nicholas, the parish clerk Absolon and Gervase the smith. Gervase makes only a brief appearance as a necessary part of the plot, but in a few lines of dialogue Chaucer gives us a picture of a bluff, hearty, honest and friendly chap, who works very hard.

The character of the rich old carpenter is sketched rather than painted. The sketch is of a conventional picture of a mean, rich old man, obsessed by the beauty of his lovely young wife. But in the course of the story there are glimpses of a real and human person. He is, indeed, a suspicious and jealous old man who is mean enough to restrict the freedom of his young wife, 'heeld hire narwe in cage', and yet for all his ignorance and gullibility, he is honest and loyal. He is genuinely worried about Nicholas's non-appearance and his assumed malady, and in his ignorant and rather pathetic way he does what he can to effect a cure. One can see him with ever-widening eyes, listening horror-struck to Nicholas's fore-cast of impending doom, and there is something pathetic in the foreboding cry 'Allas, my wyf!' Although he may seem ridiculous, there is tragi-comedy in his desperate attempts to complete the secret preparations for the escape, in the lodging in the tub and the final awakening, the cutting of ropes and the crashing to the floor; incurring at the last a broken arm and ridicule. His 'faults' are that he was foolish to marry so young a wife, and mean to be jealous, and it is poetic justice that he should be both deceived and ridiculed.

The portrait of Alison is built up with touches of vivid colour and fine detail, in what appears at first sight to be a casual and random manner. Her picture is developed by a series of striking images which are unusual in their basic homeliness and exciting in their appropriateness – the blossom in spring, a newly minted gold coin, a weasel, a kid, calf and restless young colt, mead and honey and apples. By the use of such imagery, the portrait of a lovely young girl, attractively (and indeed richly) dressed in black and white with matching decoration, is made to live and move with a warm sensuality that is almost magical. Alison's characterization is mainly decorative, but none the less important to the plot, for three reasons: firstly, to emphasize the ridiculous position of the jealous old husband trying to keep in his control the obvious desirability of his lovely young wife; secondly, as a natural conquest for Nicholas and, therefore, a good reason for the plot of deception; and thirdly, as a perfect target for Absolon's artificial and ridiculous love affair. Decorative though she may be, there are glimpses of a shrewd and confident 'young madam' – in her love affair with Nicholas, in the play-acting with her husband and in her treatment of poor Absolon.

Nicholas is the 'hero' of *The Miller's Tale*, the good-looking, well-educated, quietly confident man-of-the-world; living comfortably in private rooms in a nice part of town, with a private income that enables him to indulge in the study of astrology. He is obviously very clever, and his wits are certainly sharp. This is witnessed by the ingenuity of his plan, and the clever psychological approach he takes to deceive the ignorant and gullible carpenter. Reserved in manner though he is, he has a strong character, and there is little subtlety about his amorous advance on Alison. Nicholas is the central character in the plot of *The Miller's Tale*, and the driving force of the action. The man-of-action image is emphasized by there being no detailed physical portrait of Nicholas. In this central position he acts as a foil to Absolon, emphasizing by his direct and ruthless approach the weakness of character, the prim fastidiousness and superficiality of the parish clerk; but also as the contrast for Chaucer to satirize the romantic world of courtly love so brilliantly portrayed in the character and behaviour of Absolon.

Absolon is the most interesting of all the characters in the tale: he is portrayed with a detail and complexity not matched in the other portraits. Absolon's part in the tale, though peripheral to the main theme, is extensive and crucial, adding the piquant sauce of exquisite irony and satire to the boisterous gravy of the comedy. In portrait-painting, his description is as vivid and detailed as that of Alison's; the effeminate young fop, fastidious in appearance and habits, over-dressed to the point of ridicule, 'with poules window corven on his shoes'. Apart from self-adoration, his energies are taken up in self-advertisement, in socializing and in flirting; and in making himself useful in such activities where company and gossip are the essential ingredients – in the barber shop, in simple legal matters and in the local drama. He likes to be the centre of attraction, as when carrying around the censer in church, and he delights in playing at being in love with the parish wives and barmaids of the town. His fastidiousness, his toilet preparations, his cultivated and refined manner of speaking, and his acute sensitivity, all combine to present a figure ridiculously out of place in the vital and vulgar setting of the tale. In his wooing of Alison he is in every way the ridiculous counterpart of the smooth Nicholas. With his high-pitched refined choir-boy voice and his indirect approach and elaborate language, he represents a complete satire of 'courtly love' (making love by the book) which is ridiculous in the context, and in sharp contrast to the amorality and physically direct sensuality of Nicholas and Alison. Absolon's feeling of insecurity makes him a pathetic and ineffective character, and leads to his comic and tragic ridicule.

In our modern way we can easily find sympathy for both Absolon and the carpenter, but this is to misunderstand the whole point of the story, which is so succinctly put in the last five lines. There is poetic justice in the final result; all the characters get what they deserve, and that is how a good story should end.

The Miller's Tale in Chaucer's Middle English with a translation into Modern English

The Portrait of the Miller
from *The General Prologue*, lines 547–68

The Millere was a stout carl for the nones;
Ful big he was of brawn, and eek of bones.
That proved wel, for over al ther he cam,
At wrastlinge he wolde have alwey the ram.
He was short-sholdred, brood, a thikke knarre;
Ther was no dore that he nolde heve of harre,
Or breke it at a renning with his heed.
His berd as any sowe or fox was reed,
And therto brood, as though it were a spade.
Upon the cop right of his nose he hade
A werte, and theron stood a toft of heris,
Reed as the brustles of a sowis eris;
His nosethirles blake were and wide.
A swerd and bokeler bar he by his side.
His mouth as greet was as a greet forneys.
He was a janglere and a goliardeys,
And that was moost of sinne and harlotries.
Wel koude he stelen corn and tollen thries;
And yet he hadde a thombe of golde, pardee.
A whit cote and a blew hood wered he.
A baggepipe wel koude he blowe and sowne,
And therwithal he broghte us out of towne.

Translation

The Miller was a stout fellow, big in brawn and bones – which stood him in good stead: he always won the prize at wrestling matches. A broad, thick-set fellow with short upper arms, he could heave any door off its hinges, or run at it and break it in with his head. His beard was red as any sow or fox, and broad, too – shaped like a spade. On the very tip of his nose he had a wart, on which there stood a tuft of hairs, red as the bristles of a sow's ear; and his nostrils were black and wide. At his side he wore a sword and small shield. His mouth was as large as a great furnace. He was a noisy buffoon and foul-mouthed teller of disreputable tales. He was clever at stealing corn and getting three times his due for grinding it. He had a thumb of gold, by God. He wore a white coat and blue hood. He blew well at the bagpipes and made a good sound, with which he led us out of town.

The Miller's Prologue

Heere folwen the wordes bitwene the Hoost and the Millere.

Whan that the Knight had thus his tale ytoold,   1–11
In al the route nas ther yong ne oold
That he ne seide it was a noble storie,
And worthy for to drawen to memorie;
And namely the gentils everichon.
Oure Hooste lough and swoor, 'So moot I gon,
This gooth aright; unbokeled is the male.
Lat se now who shal telle another tale;
For trewely the game is wel bigonne.
Now telleth ye, sir Monk, if that ye konne
Somwhat to quite with the Knightes tale.'
   The Millere, that for dronken was al pale,   12–19
So that unnethe upon his hors he sat,
He nolde avalen neither hood ne hat,
Ne abide no man for his curteisie,
But in Pilates vois he gan to crie,
And swoor, 'By armes, and by blood and bones,
I kan a noble tale for the nones,
With which I wol now quite the Knightes tale'.
   Oure Hooste saugh that he was dronke of ale,   20–27
And seide, 'Abyd, Robin, my leeve brother;
Som bettre man shal telle us first, another.
Abyd, and lat us werken thriftily.'
   'By Goddes soule,' quod he, 'that wol nat I;
For I wol speke, or elles go my wey.'
   Oure Hoost answerde, 'Tel on, a devel wey!
Thou art a fool; thy wit is overcome.'

The Miller's Prologue

Here follow the words betwixt the Host and the Miller.

  When the Knight had told his tale, there was no one in the party, young or old, who disagreed that it was indeed a noble story and worthwhile to remember, particularly the more educated companions. Our Host laughed and exclaimed, 'As I may prosper, this is going well! We've opened up the bag of tales now! Let's see who is going to tell another tale? My goodness, the game has started well! Now, Sir Monk, see if you can tell something to match the Knight's tale.'

  The Miller, who was very pale, and was so drunk that he could not easily sit on his horse, was not in any mood to be polite or to respect the courtesy of others. In a loud Pilate-like voice he began to shout and swear, 'By the arms and blood and bones of Christ! I can tell a noble tale which will match the tale of the Knight!'

  Our host could see that he was drunk, and said, 'Wait a minute, Robin, my good brother! Someone more respectable should first tell us another tale. Hold on, and let us organize this properly!'

  'By God's Soul!' the Miller said, 'that I will not! For I will tell my tale now, or else I shall go off on my own!'

  Our host answered, 'Oh, tell on then, and may the devil take you! You are a fool, and you are certainly not in any fit state!'

'Now herkneth,' quod the Millere, 'alle and some!   28–35
But first I make a protestacioun
That I am dronke, I knowe it by my soun;
And therfore if that I misspeke or seye,
Wite it the ale of Southwerk, I you preye.
For I wol telle a legende and a lyf
Bothe of a carpenter and of his wyf,
How that a clerk hath set the wrightes cappe.'

The Reve answerde and seide, 'Stint thy clappe!   36–41
Lat be thy lewed dronken harlotrie.
It is a sinne and eek a greet folie
To apeyren any man, or him defame,
And eek to bringen wives in swich fame.
Thou mayst ynogh of othere thinges seyn.'

This dronke Millere spak ful soone ageyn   42–58
And seide, 'Leve brother Osewold,
Who hath no wyf, he is no cokewold.
But I sey nat therfore that thou art oon;
Ther been ful goode wives many oon,
And evere a thousand goode ayeyns oon badde.
That knowestow wel thyself, but if thou madde.
Why artow angry with my tale now?
I have a wyf, pardee, as wel as thow;
Yet nolde I, for the oxen in my plogh,
Take upon me moore than ynogh,
As demen of myself that I were oon;
I wol bileve wel that I am noon.
An housbonde shal nat been inquisitif
Of Goddes privetee, nor of his wyf.
So he may finde Goddes foison there,
Of the remenant nedeth nat enquere.'

'Now all of you listen to what I have to say,' the Miller said, 'but before I start, I admit that I am drunk – I know that from the way I speak. Therefore, if I should stutter or mispronounce, blame it on the Southwark ale, I beg you. I am going to tell you a story about an episode in the life of a carpenter and his wife, and how a student came to seduce . . .'

'Shut your mouth!' the Reeve snapped, 'lay off your drunken and obscene dirty stories! It is both immoral and stupid to slander or defame any man, or to slander wives in general, when there are so many other things that you could tell us about!'

This drunken Miller snapped back at once and said, 'My dear brother Oswald, he who has no wife cannot be a cuckold! That is not to say, however, that you are one. There are a great many honest women around – in fact a thousand good ones for every bad one! You know this yourself only too well, unless you are crazy. Why are you so angry about my story? By God, I have a wife the same as you, and yet, for all the oxen in my plough, I would not assume so much as to judge whether or not I am a cuckold. Although I am jolly sure I'm not! A husband should not be too inquisitive either of God's secrets or those of his wife. As God's plenty is all around us for the taking, there is no need to worry about the small things!'

What sholde I moore seyn, but this Millere   59–78
He nolde his wordes for no man forbere,
But tolde his cherles tale in his manere.
M'athinketh that I shal reherce it heere.
And therfore every gentil wight I preye,
For Goddes love, demeth nat that I seye
Of ivel entente, but for I moot reherce
Hir tales alle, be they bettre or werse,
Or elles falsen som of my mateere.
And therfore, whoso list it nat yheere,
Turne over the leef and chese another tale;
For he shal finde ynowe, grete and smale,
Of storial thing that toucheth gentillesse,
And eek moralitee and hoolinesse.
Blameth nat me if that ye chese amis.
The Millere is a cherl, ye knowe wel this;
So was the Reve eek and othere mo,
And harlotrie they tolden bothe two.
Aviseth yow, and put me out of blame;
And eek men shal nat maken ernest of game.

What more can I say? This Miller was not prepared to stop talking for anyone, but proceeded to tell his scurrilous tale in his own churlish way. I feel, however, that I should faithfully set down all that he said. Therefore, for God's sake, I pray that every person of sensitive nature shall not judge what I relate as purposely obscene, but only from the standpoint that I am bound to repeat every word of his story, be it good or bad, or else prove false to my sources. Therefore, whoever may wish to avoid hearing about this, should turn over the page and choose another story. He shall indeed find enough types of stories, both long and short, which are concerned with romance, morality and holiness. Please do not blame me if you should choose badly. The Miller is a knave, you know that only too well – so is the Reeve (and some others too), and they both tell dirty stories. Think about this and do not criticize me, just as one would not be expected to take seriously what is intended as fun.

The Miller's Tale

Heere biginneth the Millere his tale.

Whilom ther was dwellinge at Oxenford   79–90
A riche gnof, that gestes heeld to bord,
And of his craft he was a carpenter.
With him ther was dwellinge a poure scoler,
Hadde lerned art, but al his fantasie
Was turned for to lerne astrologie,
And koude a certein of conclusiouns,
To demen by interrogaciouns,
If that men asked him in certein houres
Whan that men sholde have droghte or elles shoures,
Or if men asked him what sholde bifalle
Of every thing; I may nat rekene hem alle.

This clerk was cleped hende Nicholas.   91–109
Of deerne love he koude and of solas;
And therto he was sleigh and ful privee,
And lyk a maiden meke for to see.
A chambre hadde he in that hostelrie
Allone, withouten any compaignie,
Ful fetisly ydight with herbes swoote;
And he himself as sweete as is the roote
Of licoris, or any cetewale.
His Almageste, and bookes grete and smale,
His astrelabie, longinge for his art,
His augrim stones, layen faire apart,
On shelves couched at his beddes heed;
His presse ycovered with a falding reed;
And al above ther lay a gay sautrie,
On which he mad a-nightes melodie
So swetely that all the chambre rong;
And *Angelus ad virginem* he song;
And after that he song the Kinges Noote.

The Miller's Tale

Here begins the Miller's Tale.

  Once there lived in Oxford a rich old codger who was by trade a carpenter, and who took in lodgers. Lodging with him was a poor scholar who had studied for an arts Degree; although all his interest was now directed towards studying astrology. By investigation and experiment he was able to forecast the likely outcome of certain actions (for instance), if someone were to ask him, at a particular time, whether the weather would become dry or wet; or if he were asked what was likely to happen in other varying circumstances. I can't remember them all.

  This student was called 'Gentle' Nicholas. He had had a lot of experience in affairs of the heart and love-making, and as a result he was sly and secretive. In looks he was girlish, and in manner reserved. He had a room in the house all to himself which was attractively decorated with sweet-smelling herbs. Indeed, he himself was as sweet-smelling as a root of liquorice or any fragrant herb. His big treatise on astrology, several books of varying sizes, his astrolabe (which belonged to his study of science), his Arabic counters (placed carefully apart), all lay on the shelves at the head of his bed. His cupboard was covered in a coarse red cloth, and above everything lay his bright psaltery on which he played melodiously at night with such a sweet touch that all the room echoed with the sound. He sung the song 'The Angel to the Virgin', and after that he sang 'The King's Tune'.

Ful often blessed was his mirie throte. 110–12
And thus this sweete clerk his time spente
After his freendes finding and his rente.

This carpenter hadde wedded newe a wyf, 113–24
Which that he lovede moore than his lyf;
Of eighteteene yeer she was of age.
Jalous he was, and heeld hire narwe in cage,
For she was wilde and yong, and he was old,
And demed himself been lik a cokewold.
He knew nat Catoun, for his wit was rude,
That bad man sholde wedde his similitude.
Men sholde wedden after hire estaat,
For youthe and elde is often at debaat.
But sith that he was fallen in the snare,
He moste endure, as oother folk, his care.

  Fair was this yonge wyf, and therwithal 125–43
As any wezele hir body gent and smal.
A ceint she werede, barred al of silk,
A barmcloth eek as whit as morne milk
Upon hir lendes, ful of many a goore.
Whit was hir smok, and broiden al bifoore
And eek bihinde, on hir coler aboute,
Of col-blak silk, withinne and eek withoute.
The tapes of hir white voluper
Were of the same suite of hir coler;
Hir filet brood of silk, and set ful hye.
And sikerly she hadde a likerous ye;
Ful smale ypulled were hire browes two,
And tho were bent and blake as any sloo:
She was ful moore blisful on to see
Than is the newe pere-jonette tree, ·
And softer than the wolle is of a wether.
And by hir girdel heeng a purs of lether,
Tasseled with silk, and perled with latoun.

He was often applauded for his merry voice. In such a way this charming student was able to spend his time because of financial support from his friends and his own private income.

This carpenter had recently married a young wife of eighteen years of age, whom he loved more than his life. Yet he was a jealous man and took pains to limit her freedom, because she was young and headstrong, and he was old, and he was afraid that someone would seduce her. He knew nothing of Cato (for his intelligence was limited) who said that each man should marry someone of similar temperament; and further, that men should marry only someone of their own social level and age group, because youth and age are often in conflict. But since he had fallen into this trap, he would just have to get used to the problems, as other people have had to.

This young wife was most attractive, with a shapely and slim body like a weasel. She wore a girdle of striped silk, and to deck her loins an apron full of pleats and white as the morning milk. Her smock was also white and embroidered on the collar with coal-black silk, both in front and behind, and inside and outside. The ribbons of her white headdress matched her collar. She wore a broad silk head-band which was set rather high. Her eyebrows, which were as black as sloes, were plucked into high curves; and she certainly had a lecherous gleam in her eye. She was even more beautiful to look at than the blossom of the sweet pear tree in the spring, and her skin was softer than sheep's wool. From her girdle hung a leather purse with silk tassels and metal ornaments like pearls.

In al this world, to seken up and doun,
There nis no man so wys that koude thenche   144–50
So gay a popelote or swich a wenche.
Ful brighter was the shining of hir hewe
Than in the Tour the noble yforged newe.
But of hir song, it was as loude and yerne
As any swalwe sittinge on a berne.

Therto she koude skippe and make game,   157–62
As any kide of calf folwinge his dame.
Hir mouth was sweete as bragot or the meeth,
Or hoord of apples leyd in hey or heeth.
Winsinge she was, as is a joly colt,
Long as a mast, and upright as a bolt.
A brooch she baar upon hir lowe coler,
As brood as is the boos of a bokeler.
Hir shoes were laced on hir legges hye,
She was a primerole, a piggesnie,
For any lord to leggen in his bedde,
Or yet for any good yeman to wedde.

Now, sire, and eft, sire, so bifel the cas,   163–73
That on a day this hende Nicholas
Fil with this yonge wyf to rage and pleye,
Whil that hir housbonde was at Oseneye,
As clerkes ben ful subtil and ful queynte;
And prively he caughte hire by the queynte,
And seyde, 'Ywis, but if ich have my wille,
For deerne love of thee, lemman, I spille.'
And heeld hire harde by the haunchebones,
And seide, 'Lemman, love me al atones,
Or I wol dyen, also God me save!'

And she sproong as a colt dooth in the trave,   174–6
And with hir heed she wryed faste awey,
And seide, 'I wol nat kisse thee, by my fey!

Nowhere in the world could you find anyone with such a vivid imagination who could dream up such a lovely picture as this young poppet. Her colouring was brighter than that of a shining new-minted coin; and as for her voice, it was as full-throated and thrilling as that of a swallow sitting on a barn.

In addition, she could skip about and play a game like a kid or calf behind its mother. Her mouth was as sweet as mead or honey, or as a hoard of apples lying in the hay. She was as excitable as a restless colt, tall as a mast and straight as an arrow. On her low neckline she wore a brooch as big as any boss on a shield. Her shoes were laced high up on her calves. She was indeed a primrose, a proper darling, ripe for any lord to take to bed, or for a sturdy yeoman to marry.

Now, good people all, it so happened that one day this charming Nicholas, as students will do in their special and naughty way, started to get fresh and fool around with the young wife whilst her husband was away on business at Oseney. He grabbed at her crotch, exclaiming, 'My dearest, I will be destroyed by my hunger to love you unless I can have what I desire!' He held her tight by the buttocks and cried out, 'My dearest, let me love you now or, God save me, I will be done for!'

She shied like a colt being shod, and violently twisted her head away from him, crying, 'By my faith, I will not kiss you!

Why, lat be,' quod she, 'lat be, Nicholas,   177–85
Or I wol crie "out, harrow" and "allas"!
Do wey youre handes, for youre curteisie!'

  This Nicholas gan mercy for to crye,
And spak so faire, and profred him so faste,
That she hir love him graunted atte laste,
And swoor hir ooth, by Seint Thomas of Kent,
That she wol been at his comandement,
Whan that she may hir leiser wel espie.

  'Myn housbonde is so ful of jalousie   186–203
That but ye waite wel and been privee,
I woot right wel I nam but deed,' quod she.
'Ye moste been ful deerne, as in this cas.'
  'Nay, therof care thee noght,' quod Nicholas.
'A clerk hadde litherly biset his while,
But if he koude a carpenter bigile.'
  And thus they been accorded and ysworn
To waite a time as I have told biforn.
Whan Nicholas had doon thus everideel,
And thakked hire aboute the lendes weel,
He kiste hire sweete and taketh his sautrie,
And pleyeth faste, and maketh melodie.

  Thanne fil it thus, that to the parissh chirche,
Cristes owene werkes for to wirche,
This goode wyf went on an haliday.
Hir forheed shoon as bright as any day,
So was it wasshen whan she leet hir werk.

Now was ther of that chirche a parissh clerk,   204–11
The which that was ycleped Absolon.
Crul was his heer, and as the gold it shoon,
And strouted as a fanne large and brode;
Ful streight and evene lay his joly shode.
His rode was reed, his eyen greye as goos.
With Poules window corven on his shoos,
In hoses rede he wente fetisly.

Now, leave off, Nicholas, or I will scream "murder" and "help"! Take your hands away from me and behave yourself!'

Nicholas began to utter soft words of pleading, and was so convincing and so pressing in his manner that she surrendered and accepted his advances, promising in the name of Thomas à Becket that she would give him what he wanted when she could find a suitable opportunity.

'My husband is so full of jealousy,' she said, 'that unless you are patient and discreet, I am sure that he will kill me! Because of this, you really must be circumspect.'

'Don't worry yourself about it,' Nicholas answered, 'a student would not be using his wits properly if he could not find a way to deceive an old carpenter!'

And thus they agreed and promised to bide their time, as I have mentioned earlier. When Nicholas had finished playing around, and had had his fill of stroking her about the thighs, he kissed her affectionately, took up his psaltery and played away, strumming some tunes.

Now it came to pass that this good wife went one holy-day to the local parish church to make her devotions. Her forehead shone as bright as day, for she had scrubbed herself after finishing her housework.

There was a parish clerk at this church who was called Absolon. His hair was curly and gleamed like gold, jutting forward in the manner of a large, wide fan; and straight down the middle was a splendid parting. His complexion was rosy, and his eyes as grey as the goose. He went about fashionably dressed in red stockings, with patterns like the big window in St Paul's carved on his shoes.

Yclad he was ful smal and proprely   212–16
Al in a kirtel of a light waget;
Ful faire and thikke been the pointes set.
And therupon he hadde a gay surplis
As whit as is the blosme upon the ris.

A mirie child he was, so God me save.   217–23
Wel koude he laten blood and clippe and shave,
And maken a chartre of lond or acquitaunce.
In twenty manere koude he trippe and daunce
After the scole of Oxenforde tho,
And with his legges casten to and fro,
And pleyen songes on a smal rubible;
Therto he song som time a loud quinible;   224–43
And as wel koude he pleye on a giterne.
In al the toun nas brewhous ne taverne
That he ne visited with his solas,
Ther any gailard tappestere was.
But sooth to seyn, he was somdeel squaymous
Of farting, and of speche daungerous.

   This Absolon, that jolif was and gay,   231–43
Gooth with a sencer on the haliday,
Sensinge the wives of the parisshe faste;
And many a lovely look on hem he caste,
And namely on this carpenteris wyf.
To looke on hire him thoughte a mirie lyf,
She was so propre and sweete and likerous.
I dar wel seyn if she hadde been a mous,
And he a cat, he wolde hire hente anon.
This parissh clerk, this joly Absolon,
Hath in his herte swich a love-longinge
That of no wyf took he noon offringe;
For curteisie, he seide, he wolde noon.

He dressed fastidiously and most properly in a coat of light blue cloth, thickly provided with fastenings. Over this, he wore a splendid surplice as white as blossom on the branch.

A gay young chap he was, as God be my witness! He was experienced in bloodletting, haircutting and shaving, as well as drawing up conveyances and deeds of settlement. He could jig and dance in twenty different ways – though all in the style of Oxford – casting his legs about all over the place. He could play tunes on a small fiddle; Sometimes he sang to it in a high-pitched treble voice; and he could play a guitar as well. There was not a single tavern or bar in the town where there were attractive barmaids which he had not visited to provide some entertainment. But to be quite honest, he was rather particular of speaking, as well as being somewhat squeamish about farting.

This gay and jolly chap Absolon used to carry the censer round in the church on holy days with which he eagerly sprayed incense over the parish women, at all of whom he made eyes, particularly at the carpenter's wife. Making eyes at her, he thought, was good fun, especially as she looked so prim and sweet and sexy. I dare say that if she had been a mouse, and he a cat, he would have pounced on her soon enough. This parish clerk, jolly young Absolon, was so concerned with flirting that he would not take the collection from any of the women – he said that he would not take anything because it wasn't polite.

The moone, whan it was night, ful brighte shoon,   244–55
And Absolon his giterne hath ytake,
For paramours he thoghte for to wake.
And forth he gooth, jolif and amorous,
Til he cam to the carpenters hous
A litel after cokkes hadde ycrowe,
And dressed him up by a shot-windowe
That was upon the carpenteris wal.
He singeth in his vois gentil and smal,
'Now, deere lady, if thy wille be,
I praye yow that ye wole rewe on me,'
Ful wel acordaunt to his giterninge.

This carpenter awook, and herde him singe,   256–61
And spak unto his wyf, and seide anon,
'What! Alison! herestow nat Absolon,
That chaunteth thus under oure boures wal?'
And she answerde hir housbonde therwithal,
'Yis, God woot, John, I heere it every deel.'

This passeth forth; what wol ye bet than weel?   262–74
Fro day to day this joly Absolon
So woweth hire that him is wo bigon.
He waketh al the night and al the day;
He kembeth his lokkes brode, and made him gay;
He woweth hire by meenes and brocage,
And swoor he wolde been hir owene page;
He singeth, brokkinge as a nightingale;
He sente hire piment, meeth, and spiced ale,
And wafres, piping hoot out of the gleede;
And, for she was of town, he profred meede.
For som folk wol ben wonnen for richesse,
And somme for strokes, and somme for gentillesse.

Somtime, to shewe his lightnesse and maistrie,   275–6
He pleyeth Herodes upon a scaffold hye.

On one night, when the moon shone brightly, Absolon took up his guitar with the intention of waking up one or two of his girl friends by his serenading. So forth he went on his way, feeling merry and amorous, until he came to the carpenter's house a little after cock-crow, and took up a position by a casement window on one of the walls of the carpenter's place. He sang a song in his refined high-pitched voice, 'Now dearest lady, if it be thy pleasure, I beg you to take pity on me', keeping carefully in time with his strumming.

The carpenter woke up hearing him singing and, turning to his wife, said, 'What's this! Alison, can you not hear Absolon chanting away outside our bedroom wall?' And she replied to her husband, 'Yes, John, God knows I hear it all!'

So this sort of thing went on – what more could you expect? Day in and day out this pretty boy Absolon fell so deeply in love with Alison that he became quite forlorn. He lay awake all night, and all day he combed his thick locks and made himself look good. He wooed her by go-between and other indirect ways, and promised that he would be her very own slave. He went on singing to her, warbling like a nightingale. He sent her presents of sweet wine, mead and spicy ale, and piping hot pancakes, straight from the stove, and as she lived in the town, he tried to bribe her with spending money – for some women can be won by expensive presents, some by rough treatment and some by kindness.

On some occasions, in order to show off his skill and his cleverness, he played the part of Herod up on the wooden stage.

But what availleth him as in this cas?   277–90
She loveth so this hende Nicholas
That Absolon may blowe the bukkes horn;
He ne hadde for his labour but a scorn.
And thus she maketh Absolon hire ape,
And al his ernest turneth til a jape.
Ful sooth is this proverbe, it is no lie,
Men seyn right thus, 'Alwey the nie slie
Maketh the ferre leeve to be looth.'
For though that Absolon be wood or wrooth,
By cause that he fer was from hire sight,
This nie Nicholas stood in his light.
Now ber thee wel, thou hende Nicholas,
For Absolon may waille and singe 'allas.'

    And so bifel it on a Saterday,   291–310
This carpenter was goon til Osenay;
And hende Nicholas and Alisoun
Acorded been to this conclusioun,
That Nicholas shal shapen him a wile
This sely jalous housbonde to bigile;
And if so be the game wente aright,
She sholde slepen in his arm al night,
For this was his desir and hire also.
And right anon, withouten wordes mo,
This Nicholas no lenger wolde tarie,
But dooth ful softe unto his chambre carie
Bothe mete and drinke for a day or tweye,
And to hire housbonde bad hire for to seye,
If that he axed after Nicholas,
She sholde seye she niste where he was,
Of al that day she saugh him nat with ye;
She trowed that he was in maladie,
For for no cry hir maide koude him calle,
He nolde answere for thing that mighte falle.

But that didn't do him much good! She was so much in love with the charmer Nicholas that Absolon was quite clearly wasting his time. He gained nothing for his efforts but her contempt. Thus she made a monkey out of Absolon, and treated all his endeavours with ridicule. In fact, there is a proverb (and this is no lie) which runs, 'The sly one at hand always fares better than the good one who's absent.' For much as Absolon might rant and rave because he was far from her notice, Nicholas was always near her, and therefore put him in the shade. Now, make the best of it, smooth Nicholas, and let Absolon fret and bemoan his lot.

And so it happened that, one Saturday, the carpenter had had to go to Oseney, and Nicholas and Alison agreed on a course of action whereby Nicholas would devise a plan to deceive this stupid jealous old husband; and if the plans worked out all right, she would then be able to sleep with Nicholas all that night – for this is what he wanted, and she too. So forthwith, without saying any more (because he could wait no longer), Nicholas went quietly up to his room, carrying enough food and drink for a couple of days. He told her to tell her husband, if he should ask after Nicholas, that she had no idea where he was as she had not set eyes on him all that day. She was to say that he might be ill, as her maid had tried unsuccessfully to call him, but he made no answer at any time.

This passeth forth al thilke Saterday,   311–25
That Nicholas stille in his chambre lay,
And eet and sleep, or dide what him leste,
Til Sonday, that the sonne gooth to reste.
This sely carpenter hath greet merveile
Of Nicholas, or what thing mighte him eyle,
And seide, 'I am adrad, by Seint Thomas,
It stondeth nat aright with Nicholas.
God shilde that he deide sodeinly!
This world is now ful tikel, sikerly.
I saugh to-day a cors yborn to chirche
That now, on Monday last, I saugh him wirche.
Go up,' quod he unto his knave anoon,
'Clepe at his dore, or knokke with a stoon.
Looke how it is, and tel me boldely.'

This knave gooth him up ful sturdily,   326–35
And at the chambre dore whil that he stood,
He cride and knokked as that he were wood,
'What! how! what do ye, maister Nicholay?
How may ye slepen al the longe day?'
But al for noght, he herde nat a word.
An hole he foond, ful lowe upon a bord,
Ther as the cat was wont in for to crepe,
And at that hole he looked in ful depe,
And at the laste he hadde of him a sight.

This Nicholas sat evere caping upright,   336–44
As he had kiked on the newe moone.
Adoun he gooth, and tolde his maister soone
In what array he saugh this ilke man.
  This carpenter to blessen him bigan,
And seide, 'Help us, Seinte Frideswide!
A man woot litel what him shal bitide.
This man is falle, with his astromie,
In some woodnesse or in some agonie.

And so matters rested the whole of the Saturday, with Nicholas lying quietly in his room, eating, sleeping and generally doing what he wanted, up until the Sunday when the sun went down to rest. Then the simple carpenter started wondering about Nicholas, and about what could be the matter with him, saying to himself 'By St Thomas, I am afraid that all is not well with Nicholas. God save us, he might have suddenly died! The world, for sure, is a treacherous place! Today I saw carried to the church the corpse of someone I saw alive and kicking only last Monday!' He then told his serving-lad, 'Go up and call at him through the door, or knock on it with a stone! See what is going on and come and tell me directly!'

The serving-lad promptly went upstairs and, standing outside the door of the room, shouted and knocked as hard as he could, 'Ho there! What's up, Master Nicholas? How can you sleep in there all day long?' But all for nothing, for he heard not a whisper. He found a crack right down at the bottom of the door, which the cat used for creeping in and out, and through this crack he peered carefully into the room, at last catching a glimpse of Nicholas.

He was sitting staring vacantly upwards, as if he were moon-struck. Down went the servant immediately and told his master in what circumstances he had seen Nicholas.

The carpenter began to cross himself, and jabbered, 'Help us, Saint Frideswide! One knows so little of what may happen! Because of his "astronomy", this lad has been laid low with some madness or by some frightful stroke!

I thoghte ay wel how that it sholde be!   345–8
Men sholde nat knowe of Goddes privetee.
Ye, blessed be alwey a lewed man
That noght but oonly his bileve kan!

So ferde another clerk with astromie;   349–63
He walked in the feeldes, for to prye
Upon the sterres, what ther sholde bifalle,
Til he was in a marle-pit yfalle;
He saugh nat that. But yet, by Seint Thomas,
Me reweth soore of hende Nicholas.
He shal be rated of his studiyng,
If that I may by Jhesus, hevene king!
Get me a staf, that I may underspore,
Whil that thou, Robin, hevest up the dore.
He shal out of his studiyng, as I gesse' –
And to the chambre dore he gan him dresse.
His knave was a strong carl for the nones,
And by the haspe he haaf it of atones;
Into the floor the dore fil anon.

   This Nicholas sat ay as stille as stoon,   364–78
And evere caped upward into the eir.
This carpenter wende he were in despeir,
And hente him by the sholdres mightily,
And shook him harde, and cride spitously,
'What! Nicholay! what, how! what, looke adoun!
Awak, and thenk on Cristes passioun!
I crouche thee from elves and fro wightes.'
Therwith the night-spel seide he anon-rightes
On foure halves of the hous aboute,
And on the thresshfold of the dore withoute:
'Jhesu Crist and Seinte Benedight,
Blesse this hous from every wikked wight,
For nightes verye, the white *pater-noster*!
Where wentestow, Seinte Petres soster?'

I always well knew that it would come to this. People should not attempt to learn of God's secret ways. Yea, happy always to be an ignorant fellow who knows only his creed!

This happened to another student of astronomy. He went for a walk in the fields to look upon the stars, to see what they might reveal, and fell into a clay pit – he didn't see it! But yet, by Saint Thomas, I am very disturbed about poor gentle Nicholas. He will be told off for his studying, by Jesus, Heavenly King, that is if I have anything to do with it. Get me a pole so that I can put it underneath, while you, Robin, heave upwards on the door. He must be got out of his studying, if I can find a way!' He then got into position at the door of the room. His servant was a strong lad indeed, and he had the door off its hinges in no time, letting it fall down on the floor.

Through all this Nicholas sat fixed like a stone, ever staring upwards into the air. The carpenter judged him to be in a state of despair, and taking him strongly by the shoulders, shook him vigorously, shouting out sharply, 'Hey, Nicholas! What's going on? Look down, will you? Wake up and turn your thoughts to Christ's passion! I'll mark you with the sign of the cross to ward off the elves and spirits!' With that he recited a special prayer against spirits in all the four corners of the room, and outside the room on the threshold of the door, 'Jesu Christ and Saint Benedict, bless this house from every wicked thing and from evil spirits! White Paternoster! Where have you gone, sister of Saint Peter?'

And atte laste this hende Nicholas   379–92
Gan for to sik soore, and seide, 'Allas!
Shal al the world be lost eftsoones now?'
  This carpenter answerde, 'What seistow?
What! think on God, as we doon, men that swinke.'
  Thus Nicholas answerde, 'Fecche me drinke,
And after wol I speke in privetee
Of certein thing that toucheth me and thee.
I wol telle it noon oother man, certein.'
  This carpenter goth doun, and comth agein,
And broghte of mighty ale a large quart;
And whan that ech of hem had dronke his part,
This Nicholas his dore faste shette,
And doun the carpenter by him he sette.

He seide 'John myn hooste, lief and deere,   393–410
. Thou shalt upon thy trouthe swere me heere;
That to no wight thou shalt this conseil wreye;
For it is Cristes conseil that I seye,
And if thou telle it man, thou art forlore;
For this vengeaunce thou shalt han therfore,
That if thou wreye me, thou shalt be wood.'
  'Nay, Crist forbede it, for his hooly blood!'
Quod tho this sely man, 'I nam no labbe;
Ne, though I seye, I nam nat lief to gabbe.
Sey what thou wolt, I shal it nevere telle
To child ne wyf, by him that harwed helle!'

  'Now John,' quod Nicholas, 'I wol nat lie;
I have yfounde in myn astrologie,
As I have looked in the moone bright,
That now a Monday next, at quarter night,
Shal falle a reyn, and that so wilde and wood,
That half so greet was nevere Noes flood.

At last, this gentle Nicholas began to sigh deeply and said, 'Alas! Must all the world be destroyed again?'

The carpenter cried out, 'What are you saying? What's this? Trust in God as we do, we men who toil for our living!'

Nicholas answered, 'Fetch me something to drink, and afterwards, for your ears only, I will tell you of certain matters which concern you and me, something that I would not tell to another soul for anything!'

The carpenter went away, and returned bringing a large measure of strong ale. When each of them had drunk his share, Nicholas made the door fast shut and sat himself down by the carpenter.

'John, my host, my dear and close friend,' he said, 'upon your word you are going to swear to me here that you will not betray this information to anyone, for it is Christ's purpose that I am going to tell you about and if you mention it to anybody, then you are doomed! If you should betray me, vengeance shall indeed fall upon you for it and you will be driven mad!'

'Nay, Christ forbid, by His holy blood!' replied this simple man, 'I am no blabber-mouth! Nay, though I say it myself, I am not given to gabbling! Say what you want to, I shall never mention it to man, woman or child, by Him that harrowed Hell!'

'Now, John,' Nicholas said, 'I am not going to lie to you. I have discovered through my astrological work, whilst examining the bright moon, that on Monday next at quarter night there shall fall such a downpour, so wild and furious, that it will be twice as monstrous as Noah's Flood!'

This world' he seide, 'in lasse than an hour   411–29
Shal al be dreynt, so hidous is the shour.
Thus shal mankinde drenche, and lese hir lyf.'
  This carpenter answerde, 'Allas, my wyf!
And shal she drenche? allas, myn Alisoun!'
For sorwe of this he fil almoost adoun,
And seide, 'Is ther no remedie in this cas?'
  'Why, yis, for Gode,' quod hende Nicholas,
'If thou wolt werken after loore and reed.
Thou mayst nat werken after thyn owene heed;
For thus seith Salomon, that was ful trewe,
"Werk al by conseil, and thou shalt nat rewe."
And if thou werken wolt by good conseil,
I undertake, withouten mast and seil,
Yet shal I saven hire and thee and me.
Hastow nat herd hou saved was Noe,
Whan that oure Lord hadde warned him biforn
That al the world with water sholde be lorn?'
  'Yis,' quod this carpenter, 'ful yoore ago.'

  'Hastou nat herd,' quod Nicholas, 'also   430–48
The sorwe of Noe with his felaweshipe,
Er that he mighte gete his wyf to shipe?
Him hadde be levere, I dar wel undertake
At thilke time, than alle his wetheres blake
That she hadde had a ship hirself allone.
And therfore, woostou what is best to doone?
This asketh haste, and of an hastif thing
Men may nat preche or maken tariyng.
Anon go gete us faste into this in
A kneding trogh, or ellis a kymelin,
For ech of us, but looke that they be large,
In which we mowe swimme as in a barge,
And han therinne vitaille suffisant
But for a day: fy on the remenant!

He went on, 'In less than an hour, this world will all be drowned, so frightful will be the downpour. Thus will all mankind be drowned, and be wiped out!'

The carpenter cried out, 'Alas, my wife! Is she to be drowned as well? Alas, my little Alison!' In grief he almost collapsed, 'Is there no remedy against this happening?' he added.

'Yes, there is, through God's mercy,' replied gentle Nicholas, 'but only if you keep precisely to my instructions and advice. You must not do anything on your own initiative. For as Solomon said, who was a very wise man, "Do as you are bid and you will not be sorry." And if you do what you are told to do, I undertake, using neither mast nor sail, to save her, you and myself. Have you not heard how Noah was saved when Our Lord warned him beforehand that all the world would be destroyed by water?'

'Yes,' replied the carpenter, 'a long time ago.'

'Have you not heard also,' Nicholas went on, 'about the trouble Noah and his company had before he could get his wife on board? He would have been better off at that time, rather than having all those black sheep, I am prepared to state, if she had had a boat alone to herself. Therefore, do you really want to know what is the best thing to do? This calls for quick action, and where speed is concerned, it is not done to talk away, or hang around. Now, go and bring as quickly as possible into the house a kneading trough or a shallow tub, one for each of us. But look to it that they are big enough, so that we will be able to float in them as if in a barge! And have put in them some food, although only enough for one day – we shan't need more!

The water shal aslake and goon away   445–8
Aboute prime upon the nexte day.
But Robin may nat wite of this, thy knave,
Ne cek thy maide Gille I may nat save;
'Axe nat why, for though thou aske me,   449–58
I wol nat tellen Goddes privetee.
Suffiseth thee, but if thy wittes madde,
To han as greet a grace as Noe hadde.
Thy wyf shal I wel saven, out of doute.
Go now thy wey, and speed thee heer-aboute.

  But whan thou hast, for hire and thee and me
Ygeten us thise kneding tubbes thre,
Thanne shaltow hange hem in the roof ful hye,
That no man of oure purveiaunce spye.

'And whan thou thus hast doon, as I have seid,   459–74
And hast oure vitaille faire in hem yleid,
And eek an ax, to smite the corde atwo,
Whan that the water comth, that we may go,
And breke an hole an heigh, upon the gable,
Unto the gardin-ward, over the stable,
That we may frely passen forth oure way,
Whan that the grete shour is goon away,
Thanne shaltou swimme as mirie, I undertake,
As dooth the white doke after hire drake.
Thanne wol I clepe, 'How, Alison! how, John!
Be mirie, for the flood wol passe anon.'
And thou wolt seyn, 'Hail, maister Nicholay!
Good morwe, I se thee wel, for it is day.'
And thanne shul we be lordes al oure lyf
Of al the world, as Noe and his wyf.

The water will go down and drain away about nine in the morning of the next day. But, Robin, your servant, must not know of this, nor your maid Jill, for I cannot save them.

'Do not ask me why, for even if you do ask me, I will not disclose God's secrets! Let this satisfy you – unless you are out of your mind – to receive as great an act of grace as Noah had. I will save your wife, without any doubt. Now, go off and hurry about your business!

When you have obtained these three kneading tubs, for the three of us, then you must hang them high in the roof so that nobody sees our preparations.

'And when you have done all this, as I have explained, and have placed our food in them as well as an axe to chop the rope apart, break open a hole above you in that gable so that, when the water comes, we may escape over the stable towards the garden, and make our way out without hindrance. When the great storm has passed away, I promise that you will float as happily as does the white duck behind her drake. Then I will call out, "Hello, Alison! Hello, John! Be of good cheer, for the flood will pass away soon!" And you will shout back, "Hail, Master Nicholas! Good morning to you! I can see you clearly now it is daylight!" Then for the rest of our lives we shall be lords of all the earth, just like Noah and his wife.

'But of o thing I warne thee ful right: 475–87
Be wel avised on that ilke night
That we ben entred into shippes bord,
That noon of us ne speke nat a word,
Ne clepe, ne crie, but be in his preyere;
For it is Goddes owene heeste deere.
   Thy wyf and thou moote hange fer atwinne;
For that bitwixe yow shal be no sinne,
Namoore in looking than ther shal in deede,
This ordinance is seid. Go, God thee speede!
Tomorwe at night, whan men ben alle aslepe,
Into oure kneding-tubbes wol we crepe,
And sitten there, abiding Goddes grace.

Go now thy wey, I have no lenger space   488–92
To make of this no lenger sermoning.
Men seyn thus, "Sende the wise, and sey no thing:"
Thou art so wys, it needeth thee nat teche.
Go, save oure lyf, and that I thee biseche.'

   This sely carpenter goth forth his wey.   493–502
Ful ofte he seide 'allas' and 'weylawey,'
And to his wyf he tolde his privetee,
And she was war, and knew it bet than he,
What al this queynte cast was for to seye.
But nathelees she ferde as she wolde deye,
And seide, 'Allas! go forth thy wey anon,
Help us to scape, or we been dede echon!
I am thy trewe, verray wedded wyf;
Go, deere spouse, and help to save oure lyf.'

   Lo, which a greet thing is affeccioun!   503–5
Men may dyen of imaginacioun,
So depe may impressioun be take.

'But one thing I must warn you about which is very important. On this particular night, after we have climbed on board the tubs, we must be very careful that not one of us utters a word, neither to call nor to cry out, except for the purpose of prayer. This is the secret command of God himself!

Your wife must hang some distance apart from you so that there can be no intimacy between you – not even in the look, let alone in the act. This is the command. Go, and God speed you! Tomorrow night, when everyone is asleep, we will creep into our kneading tubs and settle down to await the grace of God.

Go along now, I have no more time to explain any further! It is said, "Send for the wise and say nothing", and you are certainly wise enough not to need any further instruction. Go, save our lives, I beseech you!'

This stupid carpenter went on his way, muttering to himself 'Alas the day!' and told his wife about his secret information. She, of course, knew more about it than he did, especially the ultimate purpose of all these peculiar arrangements. Nevertheless, she pretended to be frightened to death, and cried out, 'Alas! go about your task at once! Help us to escape or we shall all perish! As I am your honest, true and wedded wife, hurry, dearest husband, hurry and help to save our lives!'

What a force is imagination! People can actually die of imaginings, so strongly can an impression take hold! The silly

This sely carpenter biginneth quake;   506–24
Him thinketh verraily that he may see
Noees flood come walwinge as the see
To drenchen Alisoun, his hony deere.
He wepeth, weileth, maketh sory cheere;
He siketh with ful many a sory swogh;
He gooth and geteth him a kneding trogh,
And after that a tubbe and a kymelin,
And prively he sente hem to his in,
And heng hem in the roof in privetee.
His owene hand he made laddres thre,
To climben by the ronges and the stalkes
Unto the tubbes hanginge in the balkes,
And hem vitailled, bothe trogh and tubbe,
With breed and chese, and good ale in a jubbe,
Suffisinge right ynogh as for a day.
But er that he hadde maad al this array,
He sente his knave, and eek his wenche also,
Upon his nede to London for to go.

And on the Monday, whan it drow to night,   525–39
He shette his dore withoute candel-light,
And dressed alle thing as it sholde be.
And shortly, up they clomben alle thre:
They seten stille wel a furlong way.
    'Now, *Pater-noster*, clom!' seide Nicholay,
And 'clom,' quod John, and 'clom' seide Alisoun.
This carpenter seide his devocioun,
And stille he sit, and biddeth his preyere,
Awaitinge on the reyn, if he it heere.
    The dede sleep, for wery bisynesse,
Fil on this carpenter right, as I gesse,
Aboute corfew-time, or litel moore;
For travaille of his goost he groneth soore,
And eft he routeth, for his heed mislay.

The silly carpenter was quaking with fear, really believing that he could see Noah's flood come rolling in like the tide to drown Alison, his dearest honey-love. He wept and wailed, and was depressed beyond measure. He sighed and groaned continually as he went and got hold of a kneading trough, and after that some tubs, and had them secretly sent to his house where they were hung up in the roof. With his own hands he made three ladders with rungs and uprights for climbing up to the tubs hanging from the beams. He supplied the tubs with bread and cheese, enough to last for one day, and a good measure of ale in a jug. But before making all these preparations, he had sent both his servant and his maid off to London on some business.

On the Monday, as it was drawing towards night, he shut his front door and without lighting any candles, arranged everything in order. Soon afterwards all three of them climbed up and settled themselves into the tubs, each quite a way apart from the other.

'Now, hush, and let us say our Pater-noster!' said Nicholas, and 'Hush!' whispered John, which Alison repeated. The carpenter recited his devotions. He sat quite still and offered up his prayers, waiting to hear the rain come.

As a result of rushing around earlier, a heavy sleep came over the carpenter about, I should think, curfew-time, or just after. He groaned in his sleep, for his spirit was troubled; and he snored as well because his head was all twisted around.

Doun of the laddre stalketh Nicholay,   540–43
And Alisoun ful softe adoun she spedde;
Withouten wordes mo they goon to bedde,
Ther as the carpenter is wont to lie.

Ther was the revel and the melodie;   544–62
And thus lith Alison and Nicholas,
In bisynesse of mirthe and of solas,
Til that the belle of laudes gan to ringe,
And freres in the chauncel gonne singe.
  This parissh clerk, this amorous Absolon,
That is for love alwey so wo bigon,
Upon the Monday was at Oseneye
With compaignie, him to disporte and pleye,
And axed upon cas a cloisterer
Ful prively after John the carpenter,
And he drough him apart out of the chirche,
And seide, 'I noot, I saugh him heere nat wirche
Sin Saterday; I trowe that he be went
For timber, ther oure abbot hath him sent;
For he is wont for timber for to go,
And dwellen at the grange a day or two;
Or elles he is at his hous, certein.
Where that he be, I kan nat soothly seyn.'

  This Absolon ful joly was and light,   563–72
And thoghte, 'Now is time to wake al night;
For sikirly I saugh him nat stiringe
Aboute his dore, sin day bigan to springe
So moot I thrive, I shal, at cokkes crowe,
Ful prively knokken at his windowe
That stant ful lowe upon his boures wal.
To Alison now wol I tellen al
My love-longinge, for yet I shal nat misse
That at the leeste way I shal hire kisse.

It was then that Nicholas crept down his ladder, and Alison also quickly and quietly, and without more ado, they climbed into bed together – the very bed the carpenter slept in.

Then the fun and the jigging began, and Alison and Nicholas lay together, energetically enjoying themselves and making love until the bell for lauds started ringing, and the friars began to sing in the chancel.

Meanwhile the parish clerk, that amorous Absolon (who was always so lovesick and woebegone), on that Monday happened to be at Oseney with a group of friends to enjoy and amuse themselves. He had occasion to ask one of the cloisterers very discreetly the whereabouts of John the carpenter, and he, drawing him out of the church, told Absolon, 'I don't know. I have not seen him at work since Saturday. I believe that he went for some timber which our abbot sent him for. He usually goes to the grange for the timber, and stays there a day or two. Other than that, he must surely be at home. Where else he might be, I simply cannot say.'

This Absolon, who was lively and merry, thought to himself, 'Now is the time to stay awake all night, for I am sure that I have not seen him stirring about his door since daybreak. I will take the opportunity of his absence to knock discreetly early in the morning at his window (which is set low on the bedroom wall), and then I will tell Alison all about my longing for her love – at least I cannot fail to steal a kiss from her.

Som maner confort shal I have, parfay.   573–8
My mouth hath icched al this longe day;
That is a signe of kissing atte leeste.
Al night me mette eek I was at a feeste.
Therfore I wol go slepe an houre or tweye,
And al the night thanne wol I wake and pleye.'

  Whan that the firste cok hath crowe, anon   579–99
Up rist this joly lovere Absolon,
And him arraieth gay, at point-devis.
But first he cheweth greyn and licoris,
To smellen sweete, er he hadde kembd his heer.
Under his tonge a trewe-love he beer,
For therby wende he to ben gracious.
He rometh to the carpenteres hous,
And stille he stant under the shot-windowe –
Unto his brest it raughte, it was so lowe –
And softe he cougheth with a semy soun:
'What do ye, hony-comb, sweete Alisoun,
My faire brid, my sweete cinamome?
Awaketh, lemman myn, and speketh to me!
Wel litel thinken ye upon my wo,
That for youre love I swete ther I go.
No wonder is thogh that I swelte and swete;
I moorne as dooth a lamb after the tete.
Ywis, lemman, I have swich love-longinge,
That lik a turtel trewe is my moorninge.
I may nat ete na moore than a maide.'

  'Go fro the window, Jakke fool,' she saide;   600–5
'As help me God, it wol nat be "com pa me".
I love another – and elles I were to blame –
Wel bet than thee, by Jhesu, Absolon.
Go forth thy way, or I wol caste a ston,
And lat me slepe, a twenty devel wey!'

I shall certainly get some sort of satisfaction, as my mouth has been itching all day long, and at the very least that is a sign of kissing. Last night I did after all dream that I was at a feast. I will, therefore, go and sleep for an hour or two so that I can then stay awake and amuse myself all through the night.'

When the first cock had crowed, this jolly lover Absolon jumped up and dressed himself beautifully and fastidiously. First of all, however, and before he combed his hair, he chewed some grain and liquorice in order to sweeten his breath. He placed under his tongue a charm in the form of a lover's knot – with this he would be rendered more attractive. He made his way to the carpenter's house and quickly positioned himself by the casement window – it was low enough to be level with his chest – coughed softly and gently whispered, 'What are you doing, honeycomb, sweet Alison, my pretty bird, my sweet cinnamon? Wake up, darling love, and speak to me! Too little do you think of me in my distress, which for love of you pains me wherever I am. It is no wonder that I faint and suffer, craving like a lamb for the teat. Believe me, my darling, I have such a love-longing my yearning is like a true turtle-dove; and I can no more eat properly than a maid!'

'Get away from my window, you tom-fool!' snapped Alison, 'So help me God, there is going to be no game of "come-kiss-me" here. I love someone else (otherwise I would be in trouble!) who, by Jesus, is much better than you, Absolon. In the name of twenty devils, go away and let me go back to sleep, or I will throw a stone at you!'

'Allas,' quod Absolon, 'and weylawey,   606–9
That trewe love was evere so ivel biset!
Thanne kisse me, sin it may be no bet,
For Jhesus love, and for the love of me.'

'Wiltow thanne go thy wey therwith?' quod   610–18
she.
  'Ye, certes, lemman,' quod this Absolon.
  'Thanne make thee redy,' quod she, 'I come
anon.'
And unto Nicholas she seide stille,
  'Now hust, and thou shalt laughen al thy fille.'
  This Absolon doun sette him on his knees
And seide, 'I am a lord at alle degrees;
For after this I hope ther cometh moore.
Lemman, thy grace, and sweete brid, thyn core!'

The window she undoth, and that in haste.   619–31
'Have do,' quod she, 'com of, and speed the
      faste,
Lest that oure neighebores thee espie.'
This Absolon gan wipe his mouth ful drie.
Derk was the night as pich, or as the cole,
And at the window out she putte hir hole,
And Absolon, him fil no bet ne wers,
But with his mouth he kiste hir naked ers
Ful savourly, er he were war of this.
Abak he stirte, and thoughte it was amis,
For wel he wiste a womman hath no berd.
He felte a thing al rough and long yherd,
And seide, 'Fy! allas! what have I do?'

'Alas! Alas!' replied Absolon, 'true love has never been so badly treated. Then just give me a kiss, since I am not to be fortunate, for the love of Jesus and because I love you.'

'With this will you then go away?' Alison said. 'Yes indeed, my darling!' replied Absolon. 'Then get ready,' she said, 'I am coming along.'

Then she turned to Nicholas and said quietly, 'Watch this, and you will laugh yourself silly!'

Absolon got himself down on his knees, exclaiming, 'I am as happy as a lord in every degree, for after this I hope there is more to come. Your gracious gift, please, my darling! My pretty bird, grant me your favour!'

Alison opened the window quickly and whispered 'Have done! Come along and be quiet about it, otherwise our neighbours are going to see.'

Absolon started to wipe his mouth in preparation. The night was dark as pitch, and black as coal, when Alison stuck her bottom out of the window, and Absolon (poor chap, nothing worse had ever happened to him!) kissed her arse with gusto, before he realized what it was. He started back, thinking something was wrong here – he knew quite well that no woman has a beard, and he had felt something all rough and hairy. 'Alas! Alas!' he cried, 'What have I done?'

'Tehee!' quod she, and clapte the window to,   632–44
And Absolon gooth forth a sory pas.
  'A berd! a berd!' quod hende Nicholas,
'By Goddes corpus, this goth faire and weel.'
  This sely Absolon herde every deel,
And on his lippe he gan for anger bite,
And to himself he seide, 'I shal thee quite.'
  Who rubbeth now, who froteth now his lippes
With dust, with sond, with straw, with clooth, with
      chippes,
But Absolon, that seith ful ofte, 'Allas!
My soule bitake I unto Sathanas,
But me were levere than al this toun,' quod he,
'Of this despit awroken for to be.

Allas,' quod he, 'allas, I ne hadde ybleynt!'   645–51
His hoote love was coold and al yqueynt;
For fro that time that he hadde kist hir ers,
Of paramours he sette nat a kers;
For he was heeled of his maladie.
Ful ofte paramours he gan deffie,
And weep as dooth a child that is ybete.

  A softe paas he wente over the strete   652–63
Until a smith men cleped daun Gerveys,
That in his forge smithed plough harneys;
He sharpeth shaar and kultour bisily.
This Absolon knokketh al esily,
And seide, 'Undo, Gerveys, and that anon.'
  'What, who artow?' 'It am I, Absolon.'
  'What, Absolon! for Cristes sweete tree,
Why rise ye so rathe? ey, *benedicitee*!
What eyleth yow? Som gay gerl, God it woot,
Hath broght yow thus upon the viritoot.
By Seinte Note, ye woot wel what I mene.'

'Tee hee!' Alison squealed, and pulled the window shut. Poor Absolon slunk away in despair.

'A beard! A beard!' hooted the nice Nicholas, 'God's body, that was a good joke!'

The gullible Absolon heard every bit of this, and began to bite his lips in anger, muttering to himself, 'I will pay you back for this!'

Who now rubs and scrubs his lips with dust and sand, with straw and cloth and wood shavings? Poor Absolon, of course, who muttered over and over again, 'Alas! rather than own the town, I would give my soul to the devil to be revenged of this ridicule!' he complained.

'Alas, I could not avoid it!' His hot passion became cold and was extinguished. From the time that he had kissed that arse, he gave not a tinker's cuss for girl friends – he was now cured of his love-sickness. Denouncing girl friends over and over again, he began to weep like a beaten child.

Then with soft steps he crossed the street to a smith who was called Master Gervase. He was working in his forge on parts of a plough, busily sharpening a ploughshare and coulter, when Absolon knocked gently at the door, whispering, 'Open up quickly, Gervase!'

'What's that! Who is there?' 'It's me, Absolon!' 'What's this, Absolon? Christ's cross! Why have you got up so early, eh? Bless me! What's the matter with you? God knows, has some fancy woman got you out and set you on the trot? By Saint Neot, you jolly well know what I mean!'

This Absolon ne roghte nat a bene   664–74
Of al his pley; no word again he yaf;
He hadde moore tow on his distaf
Than Gerveys knew, and seide, 'Freend so deere,
That hoote kultour in the chimenee heere,
As lene it me, I have therwith to doone,
And I wol bringe it thee again ful soone.'

Gerveys answerde, 'Certes, were it gold,
Or in a poke nobles alle untold,
Thou sholdest have, as I am trewe smith.
Ey, Cristes foo! what wol ye do therwith?'

'Therof,' quod Absolon, 'be as be may.   675–89
I shal wel telle it thee to-morwe day' –
And caughte the kultour by the colde stele.
Ful softe out at the dore he gan to stele,
And wente unto the carpenteris wal.
He cogheth first, and knokketh therwithal
Upon the windowe, right as he dide er.

This Alison answerde, 'Who is ther
That knokketh so? I warante it a theef.'

'Why, nay,' quod he, 'God woot, my sweete leef,
I am thyn Absolon, my deereling.
Of gold,' quod he, 'I have thee broght a ring.
My mooder yaf it me, so God me save;
Ful fyn it is, and thereto wel ygrave.
This wol I yeve thee, if thou me kisse.'

This Nicholas was risen for to pisse,   690–97
And thoughte he wolde amenden al the jape;
He sholde kisse his ers er that he scape.
And up the windowe dide he hastily,
And out his ers he putteth prively
Over the buttok, to the haunche-bon;
And therwith spak this clerk, this Absolon,
'Spek, sweete brid, I noot nat where thou art.'

But Absolon cared not a bean for all this banter, and offered no response – he had his hands full of more things than Gervase knew. He merely said, 'My dear friend, lend me that red-hot coulter over there in the chimney. I have something particular I want to use it for. I'll bring it back to you in a short while.'

'Certainly!' Gervase replied, 'if it were gold itself you wanted, or a bag of uncounted coins, as I am an honest smith, you would have it. But in the name of the devil, what are you going to do with it?'

'Be that as maybe', replied Absolon, 'I will tell you all about it tomorrow.' With that he caught the coulter by the cool steel end and creeping quietly through the door, made his way to the side wall of the carpenter's house. He first coughed and then knocked at the window, just as he had done before.

Alison answered, 'Who is there that knocks so? I am sure it is a thief!'

'Why, no!' whispered Absolon, 'my dear sweet one, God knows it is your Absolon, my dearest. As God is my witness, I have brought a gold ring for you, one which my mother gave to me. It's a good one, and very well engraved. I'll let you have it, if only you will kiss me again!'

Now Nicholas had to get up to have a piss, and thought that this time he would add to the fun. Absolon would kiss his arse too before he went away. So he quickly pushed up the window and carefully stuck out his arse, cheeks and all up to the haunches. All this while, the clerk Absolon was crooning, 'Speak to me, my pretty bird! I can't tell whereabouts you are!'

    This Nicholas anon leet fle a fart,   698–707
As greet as it had been a thonder-dent,
That with the strook he was almoost yblent;
And he was redy with his iren hoot,
And Nicholas amidde the ers he smoot.
    Of gooth the skin an hande-brede aboute,
The hoote kultour brende so his toute,
And for the smert he wende for to die.
As he were wood, for wo he gan to crie,
'Help! water! water! help, for Goddes herte!'

    This carpenter out of his slomber sterte,   708–15
And herde oon crien 'water' as he were wood,
And thoughte, 'Allas, now comth Nowelis flood!'
He sit him up withouten wordes mo,
And with his ax he smoot the corde atwo,
And doun gooth al; he foond neither to selle,
Ne breed ne ale, til he cam to the celle
Upon the floor, and ther aswowne he lay.

    Up stirte hire Alison and Nicholay,   716–31
And criden 'out' and 'harrow' in the strete.
The neighebores, bothe smale and grete,
In ronnen for to gauren on this man,
That yet aswowne lay, bothe pale and wan,
For with the fal he brosten hadde his arm.
But stonde he moste unto his owene harm;
For whan he spak, he was anon bore doun
With hende Nicholas and Alisoun.
They tolden every man that he was wood,
He was agast so of Nowelis flood
Thurgh fantasie, that of his vanitee
He hadde yboght him kneding tubbes thre,
And hadde hem hanged in the roof above;
And that he preyed hem, for Goddes love,
To sitten in the roof, *par compaignie*.

Then Nicholas let fly with a fart. It was like a thunder-clap, with such a force that the blast almost blinded Absolon. Nevertheless, he was prepared with the red-hot coulter, which he shoved right up in the middle of Nicholas's arse.

The red-hot coulter seared his bottom to such a degree that a piece of skin, about the size of a hand, shrivelled off; and so great was the pain that he thought he was about to die. He cried out in agony, as if he were going mad, 'Help! Water! Water! For God's sake, help!'

The carpenter started from his sleep, and hearing somebody shout out 'water', thought to himself, 'Help, now Noah's flood is coming!' He then sat up and without more ado, hacked the ropes in two with his axe. Down came everything. With no time at all to take care of the bread and ale, he landed with a thump on the ground, and lay there knocked out on the floor.

Alison and Nicholas leapt out into the street, yelling 'Help! Murder!' All the neighbours came running in to stare at the poor man lying there knocked out, white as a sheet, for he had broken his arm in the fall. The poor chap now stood to fare worse in his injury, because when he tried to explain, he was immediately interrupted by Alison and the gentle Nicholas. They told everyone there that the carpenter had gone crazy; that from pure imagination he had worried himself sick with some nonsense about another 'Noël's flood', and in his derangement he had procured three kneading tubs and had hung them high in the roof. He had then begged both of them, for the love of God, to keep him company by lodging themselves with him in the roof.

  The folk gan laughen at his fantasie;   732–41
Into the roof they kiken and they cape,
And turned al his harm unto a jape.
For what so that this carpenter answerde,
It was for noght, no man his reson herde.
With othes grete he was so sworn adoun
That he was holde wood in al the toun;
For every clerk anonright heeld with oother.
They seide, 'The man is wood, my leeve brother';
And every wight gan laughen at this stryf.

  Thus swived was this carpenteris wyf.   742–7
For al his keping and his jalousie;
And Absolon hath kist hir nether ye;
And Nicholas is scalded in the towte.
This tale is doon, and God save al the rowte!

  Heere endeth the Millere his tale.

Then everybody began to laugh at his craziness. They squinted and peered up into the roof, turning all his misfortune into one big joke. Whatever the carpenter tried to say it was to no avail, as nobody was prepared to listen to his explanation. They overwhelmed the poor man with forceful oaths, everyone believing him to be mad. Even the more educated agreed, and said to one another, 'My dear fellow, the man is mad!' And everyone began to laugh at his misfortune.

This is how the young carpenter's wife came to be laid, for all the possessiveness and jealousy of her husband; and how Absolon kissed the girl's nether eye; and how Nicholas was branded on the bum. The tale is finished, and may God bless you all.

Here ends the Miller's tale.

Chaucer's grammar

It should not be forgotten that, in point of time, Chaucer stands about midway between the days of King Alfred, who died in 899, and our own. We would therefore expect the language he wrote to represent a transitional stage between Old English and Modern English, and this is in fact what we find. There were a number of quite distinct dialects of Middle English in Chaucer's time, and it was partly owing to his prestige that his own speech gained ultimately the mastery; that, and the importance of London. Old English (sometimes still called Anglo-Saxon) was a fully inflected language, closely resembling Modern German in the variety and complexity of its terminations. Modern English has very few inflections, and those it has are very simple to learn. Chaucer's inflections are far fewer than those of King Alfred, though more than our own. What we shall see is that a very large number of the inflections of Old English are represented in Chaucer by the single letter -e, which is as a rule pronounced; in Modern English we often write the -e but do not pronounce it. This is not a complete account of Chaucerian inflection, but it will be a guide to much of his grammar and much of his versification. Some of the inflections in Old English were made by changing the root vowels in both nouns and verbs, and these changes are mostly preserved in Chaucer. But even so, as early as the poet's time, there was a tendency to get rid of irregular or anomalous forms, and to require all words to conform to pattern. We shall now indicate the normal accidence of Middle English as shown in Chaucer's work; the abnormalities will be pointed out in the notes on particular words.

Nouns

There is no standard termination for the nominative and accusative singular. The dative singular is unchanged or ends in -e, and all other cases, singular and plural, end in -es. As sometimes the nominative and accusative end in -e, it must be remembered that a final -e is not a sure sign of the dative singular of a noun. Sometimes also the -es becomes -s in a long word.

Some words have plurals in -en or -n; these are survivals of Old English nouns which had plurals in -an; we still have 'oxen' in Modern English, and a few others.

Prepositions all take the dative case.

Adjectives

A few adjectives end normally in -e in the nominative and accusative singular, but most end in a consonant. In the plural all adjectives end in -e. But when an adjective is preceded by a demonstrative or a possessive adjective, such as 'the', 'his', 'your', it has an -e in all cases, both singular and plural. This form in -e is called the 'weak' form; the uninflected singular is called 'strong'.

The comparatives end in -er, and the superlatives in -este. The ancestors of the modern irregular comparisons are, naturally, found in Chaucer.

Pronouns

These are so like the Modern English pronouns that we shall not need to say much about them. We shall not, however, find forms corresponding to our 'its', 'their' and 'them'. Instead we shall find 'his' used for persons and things, 'hir' (which is easily confused with 'hir', which means 'her') and 'hem' respectively. Sometimes the pronoun 'thou' is attached to the verb when used in an interrogative sentence. We find 'maistow' for 'mayst thou'.

The plural of 'that' is 'tho', not 'those'.

The relatives show the greatest differences from the modern pronouns. Our 'who' is not relative in Chaucer, but interrogative. We find that 'that' is the chief relative if followed by 'he', 'his', or 'him' after an interval of a few words. 'That ... he' will be translated by 'who'; 'that ... his' by 'whose'; and 'that ... him' by 'whom'. 'Whiche' is used as a relative in the singular and plural, for persons and things. We still say: 'Our Father, Which art in Heaven ...'. 'Whose' and 'whom' can be used as relatives, although 'who' cannot. 'Which?' means 'of what kind?' When 'what' is used interrogatively it means 'why?'

The chief indefinite pronoun is 'man', or 'men'. It acts like the French *on* (or the German *man*), and should as a rule be translated by 'one', 'anyone'.

Verbs

These are either strong or weak, according to the method of formation of the past tense and past participle (again as in German). Change of vowel characterizes a strong verb; addition of -ede, -de, or -te to form past tense, and of -ed, -d, or -t to form past participle indicates a weak verb.

The conjugations of typical strong and weak verbs are shown below.

		Strong: to singen	Weak: to maken
Indic. pres. singular	1	singe	make
	2	singest	makest
	3	singeth	maketh
plural 1,2,3		singe(n)	make(n)

Subj. pres.	singular	1 singe	make
		2 singe	make
		3 singe	make
	plural 1,2,3	singe(n)	make(n)

Indic. past	singular	1 song, sang	made
		2 song(e)	madest
		3 song, sang	made, maked
	plural 1,2,3	songe(n)	made(n), makede(n)

Subj. past	singular	1 songe	made
		2 songe	made
		3 songe	made
	plural 1,2,3	songe(n)	made(n)

| Imperative | Singular | sing | make |
| | Plural | singeth, singe | maketh, make |

| Participles | Present | singing(e) | making(e) |
| | Past | ysonge(n) | ymaked, maad |

| Infinitive | Present | singe(n) | make(n) |

There is a tendency for a final -n to drop off.

Adverbs

Many adverbs resemble the weak adjective, having the -e ending; others add -ly or -liche to the adjective. Those in the first group lose their -e eventually, and give us the phenomenon of adjectives and adverbs of the same form in Modern English: e.g. He runs fast, He is a fast runner.

Chaucer's pronunciation

Chaucer's English is the East Midland dialect. For a considerable time before the Conquest the language of government and literature had been West Saxon, the dialect of King Alfred's capital, Winchester. After the Conquest the French language predominated in ruling, educated and, therefore, literary circles, the various dialects of English being restricted to the uneducated. Gradually, however, in the fourteenth century the English language took over from the French language as the language of state, government and literature, and it was the East Midland dialect of London and the Home Counties, where lay the seats of court, government and the universities, that became the standard.

This Standard English was the combination of the Old English, or Anglo-Saxon, and French, and this is reflected in Chaucer's vocabulary and pronunciation. In Chaucer we find the beginning of English literature as we now know it; the acceptance of an English language, with Saxon and French words blended into an 'English tongue', understood by all people. Chaucer's works were probably intended to be read aloud to an audience – at Court or to friends. If we can learn to read Chaucer with as near the original pronunciation as possible, the wit, beauty and humour will become clearer; and at the same time the meaning of many of those words made difficult for us by archaic spelling will be clarified. A good guide is to pronounce the words of French origin as if they were French, and words of Anglo-Saxon origin as if they were German.

It would be easier, and more fun, to learn the pronunciation of Chaucer's English by listening to gramophone records of Chaucer's poetry in what is considered to be the original pronunciation. Several recordings have been made of modern scholars reading Chaucer. We particularly recommend the reading of *The Prologue to the Canterbury Tales* (Argo, PLP 1001) mentioned at the end of the Bibliography, p.6. However, it will be helpful to study the following table, which indicates approximately Chaucer's pronunciation:

Vowels
Words of English origin
Short vowels

'a' pronounced like 'a' in French *placer*; but not like 'a' in English 'cat'.

'e' pronounced like 'e' in Modern English 'men'.

'i' pronounced like 'i' in 'pin'. 'y' is often written for 'i', and has the same sound as 'i'.

'o' pronounced like 'o' in 'not'. Before letters written with a number of short strokes, like 'm, n,' and especially a combination of these two, 'o' is written for 'u', but should be pronounced like 'u', as for example, in 'comen, love, somer, monk'.

'u' pronounced like 'u' in 'pull', or like 'oo' in 'soðt'; but not like 'u' in 'duke'.

Long vowels

It is often possible to recognize a long vowel by its being duplicated in writing. For example 'taak' contains a long 'a'; 'sooth' contains a long 'o'.

'a' pronounced like 'a' in 'father'.

'e' pronounced like 'e' acute or like 'e' grave in French. Only a knowledge of the origin of the words in Old English can guide the reader to distinguish between the close and open sounds, as they are called, in Chaucer; but the former sound is usually represented in Modern English by 'ee', and the latter by 'ea'. Modern English 'need' had a close vowel in Old English, where it was spelt 'nēd'; Modern English 'mead', a meadow, was 'mǣd' in Old English with an open vowel. As an indication that these two vowels had distinct sounds, we may note that Chaucer very rarely makes them rhyme.

'i' (often written 'y'), pronounced like 'ee' in 'feel'.

'o' pronounced either like 'o' in 'so', or like 'a' in 'call'. Chaucer recognizes the different pronunciations just as he distinguishes the two long 'e' sounds. In Modern English the former sound is represented by 'oo', as in 'soon' while the latter is like the vowel sound in 'note'.

'u' pronounced like 'oo' in 'soon'.

Diphthongs

'ai, ei, ay', and 'ey' pronounced like the diphthong in 'day', though some authorities believe they were sounded like 'i' in 'line'.

'au, aw' pronounced like 'ou' in 'house'; but before the combination '-ght' like the 'o' in 'not'.

'eu, ew' pronounced like 'ew' in 'few'.

'oi, oy' pronounced like 'oy' in 'boy'.

'ou, ow' pronounced like 'u', or like 'au, aw'.

In words of French origin

Such of these words as had already become part and parcel of the everyday speech would obey the rules for the pronunciation of English vowel sounds; the others would retain the vowels of the French language, which were sounded much as they are today.

In unaccented syllables

The final '-e' so common at the end of a line and elsewhere is sounded like the second syllable of the word 'china'.

Consonants

The consonants had generally the same pronunciation as they have today, with certain slight modifications.

There were no silent consonants, unless, as some scholars believe, the 'g' before 'n' is not sounded.

'kn' is pronounced as in Modern German.

'gg' is pronounced like the 'dge' in Modern English 'ridge'.

'gh' as in Modern German may be either palatal or guttural, according to whether it is preceded by a palatal or a guttural vowel.

'ng' is sounded as in southern English 'fin-ger', not as in 'sing-er'.

'th' (initial) is sounded as in 'thin', not as in 'then'.

'ch' in words of both English and French origin is pronounced like the 'ch' of Modern English 'choose'.

'w' before 'r' is pronounced like a rapidly sounded 'oo'.

'h' in words of French origin and in words like 'he, him', which are rarely emphasized, is silent; but in most words of English origin an initial 'h' is sounded. Where the metre demands that a final '-e' should be elided before an 'h', that 'h' is silent.

Final 'f' is sounded as 'f', and not as 'v'.

Final 's' is sounded as 's', and not as 'z'.

Chaucer's use of the final -e

It is important to say something about the function of the final -e found at the end of many words in Chaucer's verse. At the beginning of the fourteenth century these were generally sounded as separate syllables, but by the end of the century they were coming into disuse. In Chaucer's verse the final -e may represent an inflexional change in a noun, an adjective, or a verb; or it may be what is left of a word-ending in Old

English. There are many explanations of this termination, and the following rules usually apply in Chaucer:

1 The final -e is usually sounded, except when
(a) it is slurred over before a word beginning with a vowel (e.g. Of deerne love he koudeand of solas): before certain words beginning with 'h'; any part of the verb to have (e.g. a clerk-hadde litherly biset his while); the adverbs heer, how, and a silent 'h' as in honour, him and hem (e.g. For for no cry hir maide koudehim calle).
(b) it is sometimes dropped in some words in common use as were, wolde.

2 The final -e should always be sounded at the end of a line.

Chaucer's versification

Chaucer's verse is not difficult to read. As Professor Manly remarks, 'The general principles of stress and movement in Chaucer's language and in his verse-patterns are, so far as we can discover, essentially the same as for present English.' The main difference is that a great many of Chaucer's words end in an unstressed final -e, -en, or -es. It has already been mentioned that the final -e of any Chaucerian line must always be pronounced (as the final -a is pronounced in 'china'), together with many other final syllables within the line itself if the verse is to scan. Chaucer was a master craftsman, with an ear for subtle rhythm, and in practice many final syllables were either slurred or suppressed altogether.

The Miller's Tale, like so much of Chaucer, is written in what are called heroic or decasyllabic couplets. Each line has ten syllables, normally, and the lines rhyme in pairs. The ten syllables in a line are divided into five groups of two syllables, known as feet. In most lines an unaccented syllable begins the foot, followed by an accented one. Such a line is 80:

À rīchė gnōf thàt gēstēs hēēld tò bōrd.

However, a long poem written entirely in such a metre would become monotonous, and it was to hearers and not readers that Chaucer addressed himself. (In Corpus Christi College, Cambridge, there is a manuscript of Chaucer's *Troilus and Criseyde*, the frontispiece of which shows the poet reading to the court of Richard II.) A common method of preventing the monotony of a long series of decasyllabic lines is to add an extra syllable at the end of the line, a practice found in Shakespeare's later plays. Chaucer adopts this practice by ending lines with a word in which the final syllable ends in an unstressed -e. An example of this is found in lines 97 and 98:

Ful fetishlȳ ydīght wīth herbes swōotē
And hē hīmself as īs the rōotē.

Each line of the couplet has eleven syllables, the last being an unstressed -e. Often the final syllable is -es, as in lines 17 and 18.

Another variant is seen in line 52, where there are nine syllables only, the unstressed syllable of the first foot being omitted:

Tāke upōn mē mōorē thān ȳnōgh

By varying the number of syllables in a line Chaucer thus adds greater freedom and variety of movement to his verse. There is also another method for varying the rhythm of a line. In each line there is a pause known as a 'caesura'. Usually it is found near the middle of the line – that is, after the fourth or fifth syllable – but Chaucer realized that the monotony which a regular position of the pause would give to a line could be overcome by varying the positioning of the caesura. We find that while the first line:

Whan that the Knight//had thus his tale ytold

has the pause after the fourth syllable, there are many cases of lines where the pause is placed sometimes nearer the beginning and sometimes nearer the end.

All these departures from a rigid standard have the effect of introducing variety into the verse, bringing with it a gracefulness and easy rhythm which did not characterize the works of Chaucer's contemporaries. A case in point is Langland, who wrote in the Old English verse-form of an elaborate alliterative structure where one of the stresses in the first half of the line must begin with the same letter as the first stress of the second half.

The opening lines from the Prologue to *Piers Plowman*, almost exactly contemporary to *The Canterbury Tales*, illustrate how far Chaucer's versification had developed.

In a sōmer sēsoun. whan sŏft was the sŏnne,
I shôpe me in shrōudes. as I a shēpe wēre
In hăbite as an hēremite. unhōly of wŏrkes
Went wȳde in this wŏrld. wondrēs to hēre.

Compare these lines with the opening lines of the Prologue to *The Canterbury Tales*, and it is easy to understand why Chaucer's poetry had been referred to as 'the liquid music of language':

Whan that Aprille with his shoures soote
The droghte of March hath perced to the roote
And bathed every veyne in swich licour
Of which vertu engendred is the flour.

Textual notes

From the general Prologue to *The Canterbury Tales*

3 **noble storie** The tale of the knight which had just been told was in the full tradition of a medieval courtly romance, with all the good manners and noble behaviour expected.

4 **for to drawen to memorie** To remember.

5 **namely the gentils** Especially the better-class pilgrims who would be more in a position to appreciate the courtly background and manners of the *Knight's Tale*. 'Namely' is not to be confused with the modern meaning.

6 **Oure Hooste** Harry Bailly, the landlord of the Tabard Inn, who acted as host to the pilgrims on their journey to Canterbury, having been elected as leader of the party and organizer of the story-telling.

So moot I gon Literally, so may I proceed – so may matters (for which I am in charge) proceed or prosper. He is pleased with the way things are going with the telling of the first tale.

7 **unbokeled is the male** The bag is unbuckled, i.e. the bag is open and the contents displayed.

8 **Lat se** Let's see.

10 **telleth ye** The polite imperative.

Sir Monk The Host's intention is clearly to organize the order of story-telling in accordance with the social status of the pilgrims. The knight was chosen by lot to tell the first story. The next in order of social importance would seem to be the Monk, but the Miller has other ideas.

11 **Somwhat to quite** Something to match:

12 **for dronken was al pale** Who was very pale from drinking too much. The prefix *for* is frequently used as an intensive.

14 **he nolde avalen neither hood ne hat** To raise one's cap was considered then, as now, to be a sign of courtesy and good manners. The Miller was rough and boorish, and was not prepared to conform to the normal courtesies. We all know the type.

15 **Ne abide no man for his curteisie** Nor to respect anyone for

their good manners. This is entirely in keeping with the character of the Miller as drawn in the portrait in *The General Prologue*, and as seen in the subsequent exchanges in *The Miller's Prologue*.

16 **Pilates vois** These are three references to the Miracle plays in *The Miller's Tale*. These plays were very popular in the fifteenth century, and were usually organized by the town guilds during festivals and holy days, portraying versions of the Bible stories in an age when the Bible could be read by few people. In the plays Pilate is represented as a loud-mouthed and violent character, who rants and raves throughout his performance.

17 **By armes, and by blood and bones** By the arms, blood and bones of Christ. Not a refined expletive.

18 **a noble tale** This is just one of the many examples of irony which add to the humour of Chaucer's work. *The Miller's Tale* is far from being *noble*.

for the nones For the occasion. Used frequently as we use 'indeed'.

22 **Som bettre man** i.e. someone of higher social class. In the *Prologue* to the *Canterbury Tales* Chaucer makes excuses for not presenting the pilgrims according to their order in the social hierarchy. As you will see, the Host is going to have his difficulties in keeping to any order of social precedence.

25 **go my wey** Go my own way, i.e. leave the company.

26 **a devel wey** The devil take you. An expression of impatience.

28 **alle and some** One and all.

29 **Protestacioun** Public pronouncement.

31 **misspeke or seye** The prefix *mis-* also applies to seye.

33 **a legende and a lyf** In Chaucer's time a *legende* particularly referred to the life-story of a saint or martyr. More irony here.

35 **clerk** Student. The word clerk in the Middle Ages meant a university student who was, ostensibly, preparing himself for holy orders (cf. cleric). In fact, the riotousness of students was a commonplace in Chaucer's day.

Set the wrightes cappe Made a fool of the tradesman. This expression carries strong undertones of adultery and cuckolding. Hence the reaction of the Reeve.

36 In the *General Prologue* Chaucer tells us that the Reeve was also a carpenter. In retaliation, the Reeve tells the next tale, in the same style and with similar ingredients, about students who 'set a cap' at a dishonest miller, seducing both wife and daughter.

37 **harlotrie** This means wickedness in a general sense, though here referring specifically to wickedness of the mind – 'dirty mind'. *Harlot* means 'rascal' or 'thief' and must not be confused with the modern meaning.

lewed Mostly means 'ignorant' but can, as here, have the modern meaning of 'lascivious', 'dirty'.

40 **fame** Renown, report, i.e. notoriety in this context.

41 There are many other things that you can talk about.

44 This is proverbial.

47 And always a thousand virtuous against one bad one. The Miller is being sarcastic.

48 **but if thou madde** Unless you are out of your mind. *Madde* is a verb. Literally, unless you be mad.

52 Take upon myself more than I should.

53 **that I were oon** One of them, i.e. a cuckold.

55, 56 This point of view would have been well understood by a medieval audience, and was certainly a point of view held by *The Wife of Bath*. There is also irony as it points to the substance of the plot against the carpenter in the *Miller's Tale*.

60, 61 Typical of the Miller's boorishness and vulgarity.

62 **M'athinketh that I shal reherce it here** It seems to me that I must repeat it here. There is the implication of an apology in this statement which follows on from the apology about the order of precedence (note line 22) of the story-tellers in the *General Prologue*. Chaucer's reasons for including the bawdy tale, in its undiluted form, are developed in the remaining lines of this *Prologue*.

65 **for I moot reherce** Because I must repeat in detail.

67 **falsen som of my mateere** Falsify some of my source material.

68 **Whoso list it nat yheere** Whoever prefers not to hear it.

70–2 *The Canterbury Tales* is a collection of stories which include romances (*gentillesse*), sermons (*moralitee*) and the lives of saints (*hoolinesse*), as well as the bawdy tales (*harlotrie*) told by the Miller and the Reeve. As the *Miller's Tale* is only the second to be told in the series, Chaucer is giving his audience an indication of the types of stories that are to come.

74 **a cherl** Churl, low-born fellow, a member of the labouring class, but, unlike carl, it implies boorishness, low-mindedness and a questionable character. Cf. Modern English 'churlish'.

75 **othere manye mo** Some others too, such as the Cook (an unfinished tale) and the Summoner.

77 **Aviseth yow, and put me out of blame** So be fore-warned, and do not put any blame on me.

78 **men shal nat maken ernest of game** One should not make a serious matter out of something just meant for fun.

80 **gnof** A slang term for 'fellow', i.e. codger.
gestes heeld to bord Took in lodgers, cf 'board and lodging'.

81 **The Reeve** Was a carpenter. *The Miller's Tale* is aimed at the Reeve, as the *Reeve's Tale* is subsequently aimed at the Miller.

82 **a poure scoler** In Chaucer's time the students at the University were usually herded into squalid lodging-houses in Oxford – the colleges, as we know them, were just being established. The students were generally miserably poor, but this description certainly does not apply to Nicholas.

83 **Hadde lerned art** He had taken the course of university studies, which consisted of grammar, logic and rhetoric (cf. Arts degree).

83–4 **al his fantasie/Was turned for to lerne astrologie** All his fancy was derived towards the learning of astrology. Astrology was for most of Chaucer's contemporaries a very real science. It was firmly believed that there was a proper astrological time for everything (based on the movement of the planets in and out of the twelve signs of the Zodiac) and even Chaucer's *Doctour of Phisik* was quite as interested in horoscopes as in medicine.

85 **certein of conclusiouns** Could determine a certain number of problems.

86 **by interrogaciouns** By various experiments, by investigation.

87 **in certein houres** At what particular times.

89–90 **what sholde bifalle** What would happen in all sorts of circumstances.

In the course of the story Nicholas pretends to use his astrological skill to forecast a flood (*shoures*) at a particular and precise time (*in certein houres*).

91 **hende Nicholas** This adjective is applied to Nicholas repeatedly throughout the tale. Hende has many shades of meaning, all concerned with gentleness, soberness, graciousness, politeness, courteousness, good breeding and good manners. Here is Chaucer's irony again, for although outwardly Nicholas looked a young gentleman, his actions and his behaviour were quite the opposite.

92 **deerne love** he was well experienced in secret love-affairs.

solas A term implying sensual enjoyment.

93 **ful privee** Very reserved.

96 **Allone** To have a room all to himself was unusual for a student, particularly a room in the house of a rich old codger. Nicholas had means, and was lodging comfortably in the better-class district of Oxford.

97 **Ful fetisly ydight** Most attractively and neatly decorated with sweet herbs.

98–9 This would be significant to the audience, particularly as the hygiene of our medieval forebears left much to be desired.

100 **Almageste** Ptolemy's treatise on astronomy. This is the name given to the work on astronomy by the Alexandrian astronomer and geographer Ptolemy in the second century AD. The Ptolemaic system, in which the sun revolved round the earth, and the planets around the sun, was accepted as the explanation for the motion of all heavenly bodies until replaced by the Copernican system in the sixteenth century. This work came to Europe from the East, its name being the corruption of the Arabic *Al majisti*.

bookes grete and smale The collection of books that Nicholas had at the head of his bed was unusual, for books in Chaucer's time were rare and expensive. It was some time before the invention of printing, and books had to be laboriously copied by hand from the original manuscript. He was clearly not a poor student.

101 **astrelabie** An astronomical instrument used for measuring the degree and altitude of the stars and planets.

longinge for his art belonging to his scientific studies.

102 **augrim stones** Stones or counters marked with numerals and used for calculation purposes, similar to an abacus. The word is a corrupt form of the Arabic word meaning arithmetic: 'algorism' (itself derived from al-Khowarazmi, the name of a mathematician).

faire apart neatly on one side.

104 **falding reed** Red-coloured coarse woollen cloth.

105 **sautrie** Psaltery. An early stringed instrument played by plucking with the fingers. It was in widespread use in the time of Chaucer.

108 ***Angelus ad virginem*** A hymn, 'the angel to the Virgin'. Nicholas perhaps feels that he has some obligation to religious activity, as a student, or clerk, was ostensibly preparing himself for holy orders.

109 **Kinges Noote** The King's tune. The identification is uncertain. It has been attributed to King William, probably referring to William the Conqueror, though Richard I, Coeur de Lion, who was poet, musician and troubadour, is a more likely candidate.

112 **After his freendes finding and his rente** Generally a student was dependent for his living on contributions (*finding*) from family or friends, or from strangers for whom he would say prayers. This was the case of Chaucer's clerk in the *General Prologue*. But not so with Nicholas, for he had an income of his own (*his rente*), so his *finding* were more likely to be gifts of money with which to enjoy himself.

114 **which that** Whom.

116 **heeld hire narwe in cage** Kept her confined as if in a cage.

118 **demed himself been lik a cokewold** Considered that he would very likely be made a cuckold. The Oxford carpenter is a typical example of the old man who marries a beautiful young girl. The type is caricatured in literature and drama

throughout the ages as the *senex amans*, the 'dirty old man'.
It was, and was meant to be, an object of ridicule. In the
next lines the point is made that such an association of youth
and age is unnatural and unsuccessful. Chaucer's audience
would appreciate the strictures, and their feelings would
always be on the side of the fresh, wild and lovely Alison,
and against the *sely* carpenter.

119 **Catoun** Dionysius Cato, the reputed Latin author of a collection of maxims which was widely current in the Middle Ages.
for his wit was rude He was not intelligent. The implication
is that the carpenter was also stupid (*sely*), because even uneducated folk unable to read books should know this one truth.

120–1 The maxim was that people, for their own sake, should choose
a partner in marriage who was not only of their own social level,
but also of their own age group. In medieval times this would
be considered self-evident, both regarding the established
social structure and for reasons of nature.

122 **at debaat** In conflict.

124 **he moste endure** He must face up to the problems, as others
have had to in similar circumstances.

126 **As any wezele** This simile, physical and sensuous, sets the
scene for the vivid portrait of the beautiful, *wilde and yong*
Alison, who moves like a young animal. In comparing Alison
with a weasel, there is the added implication of quick-
wittedness.

127 **al of silk** Silk was expensive, and clearly the rich carpenter
was prepared to spend a lot of money on his wife's clothing.
Alison's smock is embroidered with silk; she has a silk head-
band; and her purse is tasselled with silk. The references to silk
add to the sensuous description of Alison's body.

128 Chaucer describes Alison in colour terms of white and black
– white apron, smock and headdress; black embroidery, ribbons
and eyebrows – except for her golden complexion. This is
another example of Chaucer's use of homely, country similes
with all the attendant associations.

129 **upon hir lendes** Over her thighs. Very much a part of Alison's
physical attractiveness, as Nicholas fully appreciated.

many a goore Wedge-shaped piece of material let into a garment to increase the width. This cloth with all its pleats was no ordinary apron, and we can imagine it swaying like a kilt as Alison moved around, enhancing her shape.

130–2 A detailed and vivid description of the richly decorated smock. The expensiveness of the clothing worn by Alison confirmed the happy financial state of the carpenter – but more important, it gives us a further insight into the character of Alison, with her desire for fashionable, pretty and expensive things.

133 The headdress, a sort of cap, was fastened under the chin by means of tapes or ribbons, which in this case were richly embroidered.

135 **set ful hye** Her headband was pushed high to show as much as possible of the forehead, a feature considered to be beautiful in the Middle Ages, and therefore to be exposed by those in fashion.

137 **Ful smale ypulled: fully plucked** Once again, very fashionable. Alison is making good use of her husband's wealth by grooming herself in the style of the fashionable ladies of the upper classes.

138 **as any sloo** Another homely simile.

139 **ful moore blisful on to see** Even more delightful to look at.

140 **the newe pere-jonette tree** The early-ripe pear-tree. It has been suggested that the pear-tree was named from John, as the fruit ripened about St John's Day. *Newe* implies in the spring, when the blossom on the tree is at its most beautiful.

141 Unusual imagery, but nevertheless striking in its association.

143 **perled with latoun** With knobs like pearls made of a metal called latoun. Emphasis on the richness and quality of the accessories.

144 **to seken up and doun** No matter where one looks.

145 **There nis no man** There is no one. Chaucer frequently uses the double negative for emphasis.

148 The Tower of London was begun by William the Conqueror on the side of the City of London. It served as a great arsenal and a prison; it also contained the Mint and its machinery

for coining the money of the realm. Chaucer had been Clerk of the King's Works, in which capacity he was responsible for the fabric of the Tower of London.

noble A gold coin. The noble was an English gold coin first struck by King Edward III in 1344. Its value varied from one-third to one-half of a pound.

149 **of hir song** As for her singing, or as regards her voice.

150–2 These are images of the spring in the countryside, with all their associations of freshness and youthfulness; and the impression of animal vitality in the description of Alison's body being like a weasel (line 126) is further enhanced by the images of the merry swallow, the frolicsome kid and calf and the restless young colt.

153 There is double meaning here, with overtones of sexual attractiveness. Her pretty mouth is made more appealing by the sweetness of her breath, which implies proximity; and taste, by reference to bragget and mead, drinks made from ale and honey were rich, sweet and heady. The image of sweetness and headiness is further emphasized by reference to the warm, sweet and almost tangible smell of apples stored in a barn.

155 **winsinge** Restless as a young colt.

156 **upright as a bolt** Straight as an arrow. The bolt or arrow of a crossbow.

157–8 The size of the brooch is another example of affluence, and Alison's inclination to show off, particularly as the position of the brooch directs the attention to the low neckline of her smock.

160 **a primerole, a piggesnie** These are affectionate names for pretty flowers, used as terms of endearment with all the association of intimacy.

161–2 The vivid portrait of a lovely and exciting girl is terminated by a twist of social satire.

166 **Oseneye** Oseney was just outside the walls of Oxford, where in the Middle Ages there was an Augustine abbey. The present Osney district lies to the west of the City, near the railway station.

168 Nicholas's point-blank sexuality is, and is meant to be, in direct contrast to the rules and behaviour of 'courtly love', so brilli-

antly satirized in *The Miller's Tale* in the character of Absolon. It is also unexpected from the young student with the girlish appearance and shy and reserved manner. We were told earlier that he had considerable experience of love-making, but as in his portrait he seemed to have all the attributes of a nice young man, the hende Nicholas, we could be excused for expecting a more subtle approach. The contrast in character between Nicholas and Absolon is illustrated vividly and satirically during the course of the tale. The use of the word *queynte* is purposely dramatic and shocking, being typical of the Miller's *harlotrie*, and in contrast to Absolon's fastidious and 'correct' approach to wooing.

170 This exclamation of Nicholas has direct associations with 'courtly love'. The terms *lemman* and *deerne love* is the terminology of romantic love, and the statement is entirely in accord with the expected protestation of a courtly lover. The contrast between the physical action and the stylized sentiment would be both striking and comic to Chaucer's audience.

174 **in the trave** A trave was an enclosure or frame where wild young horses would be restrained for shoeing. This image is in keeping with the character and temperament of Alison already described.

175 **she wryed faste awey** She violently twisted her head away.

177 **lat be** Let be, stop it, lay off.

178 **harrow** Cry of alarm, used elsewhere in the tale (line 717). The term derives from the Harrowing of Hell, a frequent subject for the Miracle Plays.

179 **for youre curteisie** As you are a gentleman. *Curteisie* in meaning embraces compassion, decency and politeness, and is a term used frequently in reference to romantic love.

180 **mercy** Once again we have a reference to courtly love. 'Mercy' was the supplication of the lover to his adored one for pity and favour.

181 **profred him so faste** He pressed her so insistently.

183 **Seint Thomas of Kent** Thomas à Becket, Archbishop of Canterbury in the reign of Henry II, met a martyr's death in Canterbury Cathedral some two hundred years before Chaucer's day, in 1170. Becket was in the Cathedral when he

was killed by four knights on the orders of Henry II, thus making the death a martyrdom. Becket became a saint soon after his martyrdom because of the supposed curative powers of his miraculously preserved blood. In Chaucer's day, the pilgrimage to St Thomas's shrine was claimed to bring many other blessings besides the healing of ailments.

185 **hir leiser wel espie** When she could find a suitable opportunity.

190 **care thee noght** Think nothing of it, don't worry yourself about it.

191 **litherly biset his while** Would be wasting his time.

200 **Cristes owene werkes** To do service to Christ's teachings, that is to pray and to carry out works of charity.

201 **haliday** A Saint's day, holy day, holy days varied according to the saint to whom the church was dedicated. Those on the Roman Church's calendar were general, but in the countryside there were additional 'holidays' for First Sowing and Harvest, all blessed by the priest. Attendance at early Mass was followed by feasting, sports and dancing. No work might be done on these days other than works of necessity and mercy.

204 **a parissh clerk** An assistant in minor orders (i.e. not yet ordained as a priest) to the incumbent parish priest, carrying out various duties such as leading the responses in church, and preparing and carrying the censer.

206 **crul** Curly.

207 **strouted** Sticking out like a fan. Absolon was very proud of his hair. He was always combing it, and the style was clearly very special.

210 **Poules window corven on his shoes** The leather at the front of the shoes is cut in a pattern like one of the windows in St Paul's Cathedral. Very decorative, and no doubt at the height of fashion.

211 **fetishly** Handsomely, elegantly, well-attired.

212 **ful smale and proprely** Very fastidiously and correctly. Absolon's vanity is emphasized by the scrupulous care he takes about his clothes, his hair and appearance, his refined manner of speaking and his cultivated behaviour. His appearance and his actions are designed to attract attention. This is in direct

contrast to Nicholas, who is quiet and reserved, and about whom we learn little as to appearance and nothing as to his dress.

213 **a kirtel of a light waget** A tunic or coat of pale blue. *waget* means 'light blue'.

214 **thikke been the pointes set** Thickly furnished with laces.

215 **a gay surplis** A surplice is a plain white church vestment. Absolon is certainly not plain, and it is in keeping with his character that his surplice should be out of the ordinary.

218 (et seq.) Absolon liked to take part in all sorts of local activities where he could make himself useful and thereby gain attention. The medieval barber, besides hair-cutting and shaving, also carried out some simple medical treatment, such as blood-letting. Absolon was a 'clerk', which meant that he was relatively well-educated, and thus was in a position, either as a favour or to earn money, to carry out some legal work. We then learn that he was also a good dancer (in the very best style), and that he spent much of his time in the pubs of the district, chatting up and flirting with the barmaids, and entertaining the company by singing and playing on his fiddle. He was a parish clerk, and took a significant part in church services. Later we learn that he was a member of the local dramatic society. He is a gregarious character, and clearly not content unless he is in the company of others. The type is familiar to us, and the portrait of Absolon is drawn in vivid and suggestive detail. Nicholas is made of entirely different stuff, and the contrast in character between the two rivals for Alison's love becomes more striking as the story progresses.

219 **chartre of lond or acquitaunce** Land conveyance and deeds of settlement.

221 **after the scole of Oxenforde** In the Oxford style. Oxford was the centre of learning in England in the Middle Ages, and was no doubt a centre for fashion. The reference, may however, be satirical.

223 **a smal rubible** A small fiddle. The rubible was an early member of the 'viol family' of string instruments which preceded the violin. Unlike the violin, the viol was played held downwards, with the instrument rested between the knees.

224 **a loud quinible** In a high treble voice, the highest voice in

choral singing. The equivalent terminology in medieval choral music appears to be 'Quadrible' and 'Quinible', relating to early conceptions of harmony for Church music. This reference must mean that Absolon had been trained as a choirboy, an image much befitting his character.

225   **a giterne** A stringed instrument played with a plectrum, very much like a lute or guitar. In the sixteenth century it was very popular, and was often played in barbers' shops for the entertainment of waiting customers. There is no doubt that the *giterne* was very popular in Chaucer's time and was to be found in similar places, as well as in inns and taverns.

226–7   **nas brewhous ne taverne** There was not a single bar or tavern which he had not visited for flirting or for entertainment. The reference in the next lines to attractive and friendly barmaids suggests that the main object of Absolon's pub-visiting was more to do with flirting and less with general entertainment.

228   **gailard tappestere** Merry female tapster – attractive and friendly barmaid.

229–30   The portrait of Absolon, like that of Alison, is concluded with a short characteristic summary. This conclusion sums up Absolon's foppish fastidiousness, over-sensitivity and vanity. The fastidiousness and vanity suffer a mortal blow at the end of the *Tale*.

of speche daungerous A haughty and refined manner of speaking. *Daunger* means 'imperiousness', or sometimes 'disdain'. Not to be confused with the modern meaning.

232   **a sencer** Censer, a container or vessel for burning incense. The censer was originally used to 'sweeten' the (small) church atmosphere with incense. Then, on the assumption that the fragrance from the censer was of divine composition, it was thought appropriate as a divine essence for use in religious services.

233   **sensinge the wives** The censer is normally swung slowly from side to side in the procession down the church. Absolon directs the swinging censer towards the attractive wives and girls as a sign of his favour, and to get their attention.

236   **him thoughte a mirie lyf** It seemed to him a happy occupa-

tion. Absolon, unlike Nicholas, plays at making love. His pleasure comes from flirting in its most innocent form, in pretended adoration with all the conventional attitudes of 'romantic love' and indeed methods of wooing. He likes the idea of being in love, but he has neither the confidence nor the manliness for direct action. This is in sharp contrast to Nicholas's strong and persuasive character.

237 **so propre and sweete and likerous** So prim and sweet and sexy.

238–9 This is an image which emphasizes Absolon's inclination to play at love-making – 'cat and mouse' play. *Hente* means seize or catch, but the understanding is to release after catching in order to play again.

240 **joly Absolon** The adjective *joly* is applied to Absolon as *hende* is to Nicholas, and *sely* to the carpenter. Joly can mean 'jolly' in the modern sense, but it is also used to mean 'pretty' and 'attractive'. It is the latter meaning that makes sense when applied to Absolon. He was what we might call, rather disparagingly, 'a pretty boy', with all the implication of effeminacy.

243 **for curteisie** This can be translated literally as 'out of politeness he could not take their offerings for the collection', but *curteisie*, as mentioned before, has all the nuances of gentle behaviour in the context of 'courtly love'.

249 **after cokkes hadde ycrowe** After cock-crow. Not as we understand 'cock-crow' as being some time around dawn. In Chaucer's terms 'cock-crow' seems to be in the middle of the night, or the early hours of the morning. Absolon makes a similar journey later in the tale (line 579) at 'cock-crow', when the night was 'dark as pitch'.

250 **a shot-windowe** A casement window with a hinge. This window, which is to be the centre of some dramatic incidents, is on the ground floor of the carpenter's house.

252 **gentil and smal** Refined high-pitched voice – no doubt cultivated.

253–4 Here Absolon uses the terminology of the courtly lover – humble, pleading and stilted.

rewe on me The conventional cry of the courtly lover.

Alison, as we shall see, is not at all impressed by this studied wooing.

255 **ful wel acordaunt** Keeping carefully in time. A touch of satire. Absolon is more concerned with the approach itself than in the object of his approach.

262 **this passeth forth** And so it went on.

what wol ye bet than weel What more can you expect.

263 (et seq.) Absolon goes through all the tribulations and antics expected of the 'wretched' romantic lover suffering from 'love-longing'; he is falling in love by the book. The true romantic lover is expected to refuse food, lose sleep, humble himself and weep tears.

266 **kembeth his lokkes brode** Absolon, for all his depression, was not prepared to go so far as actually looking wretched.

267 **by meenes and brocage** By go-between and other indirect ways. Once again, according to the book of instruction. It was not the done thing for the courtly lover to press his suit directly, so the use of intermediaries was accepted; but strictly speaking, because the love affair had to be kept very secret (for the honour of the lady in question – *deeren love*), only the closest and dearest friend was involved.

268 **hir owene page** The proper attitude of the courtly lover is to be of service to his lady. The use of the word 'page' emphasizes the ridiculous dream-world of Absolon in contrast to the earthy, natural and vital world of Nicholas and Alison.

269 Absolon's continual serenading of Alison is referred to in line 262. Absolon likes to see himself in the romantic image of a serenading lover, his voice quivering with feeling like the warbling of a nightingale.

270–2 The gifts are very homely everyday country fare, locally brewed ale and fresh hot bread; not the type of present of the noble romantic lover, and certainly not appropriate for Alison with her obvious liking for trinkets and expensive clothes. No doubt the gifts of money are for her to buy clothes and trinkets, as she lived in a town, and therefore near shops.

273–4 Some women can be won by expensive presents, some by rough handling and some by kindness and gentleness. Proverbial.

276 **he pleyeth Herodes** He played the part of Herod, i.e. in the
Miracle Plays, which were so much a part of the medieval
scene. The part of Herod was similar to that of Pilate (see line
16), being a bullying and strutting stage character played by
actors with a loud and strong voice. Absolon's high-pitched
and refined voice, his fastidious and effeminate appearance
and gestures, all combine to make him quite unsuitable for
such a manly part.

    a scaffold hye Refers to the stage or platform on wheels, on
which Miracle Plays were performed. The wooden structure
was two-storeyed, and therefore 'high', to be more easily
within the view of the surrounding spectators. The lower plat-
forms allowed for storage place for costumes and stage
property, and for 'disguising' (dressing and making-up).

279 **blowe the bukkes horn** He might as well go jump in the lake,
or some such expression of uselessness.

281 **she maketh Absolon hire ape** She makes a monkey out of
Absolon.

282 And all his endeavours were treated with ridicule.

284–5 Proverbial, 'out of sight, out of mind'. Those who are always
nearby, and make a point of it, are more favourably placed
than those who are elsewhere.

288 Nicholas who is always near Alison, as he lives in the same
house.

289 **ber thee wel** Make the best of it.

291 From this point in the story the passage of time is carefully
counted right up until the early hours of the Tuesday morning.
This dramatic technique adds credibility to the events which
now follow, leading to the climax of the plot. It is also in
keeping with the supposed exactness of astrological prophecy
and the cleverness and efficiency of Nicholas's detailed
planning.

295 **Shapen him a wile** Devise a cunning plan.

296 **sely** This adjective, which is continuously applied to the
carpenter (cf. *hende Nicholas, jolif Absolon*) has various shades of
meaning: happy or blessed: wretched or unlucky; and good
and kind. All these shades of meaning can be applied in this
context with satirical and literal overtones. The word should

not be confused with 'silly', although our modern-meaning can certainly be applied to the carpenter.

297 **game** i.e. the plans for enjoying themselves.

308 **in maladie** Unwell.

311 **thilke Saterday** The events on the Saturday have been re-counted. Now we move to the events on the Sunday.

315 **greet merveile** Seriously to wonder about.

317 **Thomas à Becket** As in line 183.

319 **God shilde** God save us, he might have suddenly died.

320 **ful tikel** Very unpredictable, treacherous.

321 **a cors** A corpse. This is sometimes understood in the literal sense of a corpse in a shroud, i.e. of a person whose relatives and friends could not afford a simple coffin.

329 **maister Nicholay** The carpenter's servant would have treated the well-educated Nicholas with some deference.

332 **ful lowe upon a bord** Low down in one of the planks of the door.

336 **evere caping upright** Staring vacantly upwards. This is the first move in the impressive and detailed plan of Nicholas to deceive the carpenter. Nicholas is feigning the temporary paralysis resulting from sudden shock.

337 This is an allusion to the common belief that the sight of the new moon could bring about madness.

340 **to blessen him** To cross himself. It is an instinctive reaction of the pious carpenter to make the sign of the cross to ward off evil spirits.

341 **Seinte Frideswide** A prioress of the eighth century who was the patron saint of Oxford. There was a priory of St Frides-wide at Oxford, and the shrine is to be found in the cathedral.

342 **a man woot litel** One knows so little of what may happen. This ordinary remark, quite in keeping with pious ignorance, takes on the flavour of dramatic irony. Firstly, the carpenter is right to be worried, because many things are going to happen during the next day or so about which he is quite un-prepared. Secondly, Nicholas has planned exactly what is going to happen – or so he thinks! Thirdly, both Alison and Absolon are surprised by events which follow.

343 **astromie** Astronomy. A corrupted form of word is needed by the metre in this line, but it could also be intended to reflect the carpenter's ignorance.

346 **Goddes privetee** God's secret ways. Nicholas is relying on the carpenter's inquisitiveness and guillibility of *Goddes privetee* for the successful execution of his plan.

348 **that noght but oonly his bileve kan** Who knows nothing more (of these things) but his creed.

351 **what ther sholde bifalle** What events were forecasted, what would be revealed about the future.

353 A pointer to later events. This time it is the simple carpenter, who is so happy in his ignorance, who will fall down.

357 **that I may underspore** So I can thrust it underneath.

359 **as I gesse** If I can forecast anything, or if I can find a way.

370 **Cristes passioun** Christ's suffering and crucifixion. The carpenter's knowledge would have been derived from the Miracle Plays, as would also his knowledge of Noah's Flood.

371 **I crouche thee** I'll mark you with the sign of the cross. It was common practice to make the sign of the cross to ward off the demons and evil spirits which the carpenter automatically assumes are the cause of Nicholas's bewitchment.

372 **the night-spel** This refers to a special prayer, familiarly known as the White Paternoster, which was used to expel evil spirits (which were mostly imagined at night-time). The carpenter recites the special prayer five times, ônce at each corner of the room and on the threshold of the door. This would have been the procedure for exorcizing spirits from a haunted room.

375 **Seinte Benedight** St Benedict (c. 480–543) the patriarch of Western monasticism; a sixth-century monk who founded at Monte Cassino the first western-style monastery. He drew up Rules for the conduct of a monastery, which were introduced into England by St Augustine, first Archbishop of Canterbury.

377 **white *pater-noster*** Probably indicating the use of the rosary itself (called the *pater-noster*) with a large white bead, calling for a special prayer.

377–8 These lines are not properly understood. They probably represent, in a corrupt form, names and extracts of prayers or charms.

nightes verye Demons of the night.

seinte Petres soster Sister of St Peter. This lady is unknown.

381 **eftsoones** Again. The first time was Noah's Flood. Nicholas hints at his coming forecast of the next great flood. The detail, sequence and timing of Nicholas's plan is superb.

383 **men that swinke** Men who toil for their living, i.e. men who work with their hands as opposed to learned people who read books.

394 **upon thy trouthe** On your word of honour.

396 **Cristes conseil** This would be sure to impress the pious carpenter.

399 **if thou wreye me, thou shalt be wood** If you betray me you will be driven mad. There is irony here, for at the end of the story the carpenter attempts to explain the circumstances, and is considered by everyone (encouraged by Nicholas) to be mad.

402 **I nam nat lief to gabbe** I am not given to gabbling.

404 **to child ne wyf** To man, woman or child – i.e. to nobody.

him that harwed helle i.e. Christ. The Harrowing of Hell was a familiar bible story in the Middle Ages, based on the apocryphal Gospel of Nicodemus. It is the story of Christ's descent into hell to release from everlasting torture the pre-Christian patriarchs and prophets, and is one of the subjects of the Miracle Plays.

407 **as I have looked in the moone bright** The science of astronomy/astrology in the Middle Ages classified the moon as a watery planet which influenced both tides and rainfall. If the moon entered the division of one of the Signs of Zodiac at a particular period favourable to water, watery tumult of one sort or another would result.

408 **now a Monday next, at quarter night** Next Monday, a quarter of the way through the night, i.e. about 9 p.m. Nicholas's forecast is very precise. In the Middle Ages, day and night were divided into twelve hours each (clock time). Day:

6 a.m. to 6 p.m.; night: 6 p.m. to 6 a.m. – near approxima-
tions to dawn and dusk, sunrise to sunset. Hence 'quarter-
night' was 9 p.m.

419 **werken after loore and reed** Keep precisely to my instructions and advice.

422 **Werk al by conseil** Take advice.

424 **Withouten mast and seil** Without needing mast or sail, i.e.
without needing a boat. This points to the requirement of
kneading tubs only; a more practical arrangement for the
purpose and timing of Nicholas' plan.

431–2 Having mentioned the subject of Noah, and how he was
saved, Nicholas now introduces the subject of Noah's wife as a
necessary preliminary to arrangements for separating Alison
from her husband at the required time. The story of Noah's
troubles with his wife is a reference to the comic accounts
which were included in the Miracle Plays on this subject. In
one of the plays Noah's wife refuses to board the Ark until she
has finished her spinning. She is eventually forced into the Ark
by physical means. Nicholas is hinting to the carpenter that
Alison could cause him a problem.

435 **a ship hirself allone** Here Nicholas comes to an important
part of his plan, to separate Alison from her husband.

442 **Swimme as in a barge** Float as in a barge, i.e. as safely as
in a sea-going barge.

444 **fy on the remenant** The rest doesn't matter.

446 **about prime** About nine in the morning. Nicholas continues
to make precise forecasts.

447–8 Neither Robin, the servant boy, nor Gillian, the maid, have
any part to play in Nicholas's plan. Indeed, it would be more
than inconvenient if they should still be around when the time
came.

450 To emphasize the need for the servant's absence. The carpenter,
a pious and ignorant man, would be impressed by Nicholas's
mysteriousness, as we have been reminded that he did not
believe in being too inquisitive concerning *Goddes privetee*.

458 **purveiaunce** Preparations.

473–4 Nicholas is suggesting that all the worry and trouble will be

worthwhile, as they will end up as rulers of the world. This
no doubt would excite the simple carpenter, and encourage
him to carry out the instructions properly.

477 **entred into shippes bord** Climbed on board. Nicholas introduces nautical terminology to give, in the mind of the carpenter, some semblance of seaworthiness to the kneading-tubs.

478–80 Nicholas's imaginative plan has been devised in exact detail.
There must be no talking so that the carpenter will fall off to
sleep, thus enabling Nicholas and Alison to slip away. But
prayers should be said, thus keeping the carpenter's thoughts
concentrated on the impending disaster and the mysterious
power of God. The necessity for silence is underlined by the
mention of its being the particular command of God.

481–3 The ground for separating Alison from her husband has been
prepared by the earlier references to the trouble Noah had had
with his wife (lines 431–5). Now the precise arrangements are
being explained. It is implied that it is God's command that
Alison's tub must be positioned as far away as possible from
that of the carpenter, and that it is imperative that husband
and wife shall ignore each other during the vigil. Preposterous
though it may be, the imaginative and cunning plan is un-
folded with such coherence and artistry, and in such detail,
that the reader is carried away in the spirit of the adventure.

484 **This ordinance is seid** This ends the commands I have had
(from God). Nicholas comes to the end of his explanation with
the stamp of authority. He now intends that there shall be no
time for reflection or doubt, so the carpenter's mind must be
concentrated on action, *Go, God thee speede*.

488–9 **Go now thy wey** Get going, there is no more time to be
lost in explanation. Nicholas adds urgency to his call for
action.

490 **sende the wise, and sey no thing** Proverbial, call for the
wise man and leave everything to him.

491 **Thou art so wys, it needeth thee nat teche** This piece of
blatant flattery is the culmination of Nicholas's psychological
attack on the pious, ignorant and gullible carpenter. For all
the detailed instructions given to him by Nicholas, the
carpenter can now feel that he is in charge of the great rescue

arrangements, particularly as in the next line Nicholas 'implores' him to save their lives.

496 **she was war** Alison has of course been fully briefed by Nicholas.

497 **what al this queynte cast was for to seye** What all these peculiar arrangements were intended for. Queynte used as an adjective has many shades of meaning – 'strange', 'curious', 'graceful', 'artful'. In this context there are also the associations of sex as found in lines 167–8.

501 A nice touch, this. Alison is playing her part with true dramatic irony.

503 **which a greet thing is affeccioun** What a force is imagination! *Affeccioun* is a difficult word to translate into modern English. It has a wider and deeper meaning than its modern equivalent, more concerned with 'feelings' and 'impressions', 'notions', or 'flights of fancy'.

504 **of imaginacioun** From imagining things.

507 **him thinketh verraily** He really believed, i.e. in his imagination.

509–10 Perhaps we should have some sympathy for the wretched carpenter as he is thinking more of Alison, *his hony deere*, than himself. But this is to be too modern and sentimental. It is not love but possessiveness that links the carpenter with Alison, and the union is unnatural.

514–15 **prively, in privetee** The irony of the situation is now enhanced by the carpenter creeping around and doing things in secret.

524 **to London** London is more than fifty miles away from Oxford, and in Chaucer's time the journey would necessitate a long absence from home.

525 **on the Monday, whan it drow to night** In keeping with the precise timing of the plan and the astrological forecast.

529 **wel a furlong way** quite a way from each other.

530 **Now, *Pater-noster*, clom** Now hush, and let us say our Paternoster prayer. Clom is colloquial.

535 **for wery bisynesse** Remember, the carpenter had spent all day anxiously making all the arrangements and doing everything himself for secrecy.

537 **corfew-time** The time is thought to be about 8 p.m. In the Middle Ages the ringing of a (church) bell was a signal to put out all fires and uncovered lights. Houses were built of timber and all domestic fires were 'open', sparks from which were liable to cause destructive conflagrations, especially in towns. French *covre-feu*: cover the fire.

539 A vivid and ridiculous image of the carpenter twisted around in the small kneading-trough, snoring and groaning.

547–8 The bell for lauds is the first activity of the day in a monastery, when all the monks assemble in church to celebrate the first office of the day and sing hymns (lauds) of praise. There is dramatic irony here, as the first service of the day was considered as a celebration, and its reference connects the mind with the *revel* and the *melodie* of the happy union of Alison and Nicholas. The time of lauds was very early in the morning.

549 Absolon is certainly not behaving as a woebegone, wretched lover.

550 **for love alwey so wo bigon** We know that Absolon gets peculiar satisfaction by pretending that he is in love.

551 **Oseneye** See note to line 166.

559–60 It is apparent that the carpenter had a contract to work at the abbey at Oseney, as the monk states that he was in the habit of going to one of the 'granges', or outlying farms, to select and collect the timber he needed for his woodwork.

565 The carpenter has clearly been successful in keeping both himself and his arrangements hidden.

567 **at cokkes crowe** See note line 249. It has been quoted from an Elizabethan book that cocks crowed at midnight, three in the morning and just before sunrise.

569 **that stant ful lowe** As can be seen in our English villages, the ground-floor windows of medieval houses were placed low on the wall. The positioning of the window has particular relevance to the events which are to follow.

573 **Som maner confort** Some sort of satisfaction. But Absolon is expecting only some token to keep up his pretence of acting the lover. This is ironic for the *confort* he receives is to be everything that is distasteful to his fastidious character – physical, blunt and vulgar.

574–5 The forecasting of events from itching is an old and common belief. Absolon of course makes it mean what he would like it to mean. Even nowadays we hear that an itching palm foretells the coming of a gift of money.

576 Ironic. Absolon is correct in making a forecast from the itching of his mouth and his dream of being at a feast, but the event and relationship is different and unexpected.

578 **pleye** In all the senses of playing at making love. Typical of Absolon's character, and in direct contrast to Nicholas.

579 **first cok hath crowe** This must be in the early hours of the morning, for Alison and Nicholas had been undisturbed in their love-making until the ringing of the laud's bell (line 547).

581 **at point-devis** Smart in every detail, fastidiously

582–3 These toilet preparations, scented and sweet-smelling, and designed to make him pretty and attractive, underline the foppish, vain and superficial nature of Absolon's character. And that these preparations are carried out before he combed his hair, which he was in the habit of doing lovingly and often, emphasizes his vanity and self-adoration.

584 **a trewe-love** This is understood as referring to leaves of a plant called herb-paris, which grew in the form of a love-knot. Absolon uses it as a lucky charm for his planned wooing.

590–99 Once again Absolon addresses Alison in the studied terminology and sentiment of courtly love (lines 253–4), asking for a favour out of pity for his wretchedness, for his melancholy and love-sickness, and his inability to eat. All these sentiments conform to the rules for the behaviour of an 'ideal' lover and, are, in such a context, exquisitely satirical.

595 **swelte and swete** Swelter and sweat. Absolon is trying to emphasize his burning passion, but he can mean it only metaphorically, as it is not in his character to experience such physical reaction.

596 The image of the pathetic little lamb crying for its mother's teat is psychologically fitting in all respects, and emphasizes Absolon's feeling of insecurity, which is seen clearly in his make-up and behaviour.

599 The image of a young girl off her food completes the unconsciously pathetic self-description.

600 **Jakke fool** Tom fool, an expression of contempt.

601 **com pa me** Come-kiss-me. This is thought to have been the name or refrain of a popular song, or a game played by girls and boys.

602 **elles I were to blame** Otherwise I would be in trouble. Alison means to give the impression that she is referring to her husband, but she actually means Nicholas.

605 **a twenty devel wey** In the name of twenty devils. Compare the Host's remark in line 26, *a devel wey*.

616–17 **lord at alle degrees** The favour of a kiss from Alison is the culmination of all Absolon's pretentious behaviour as a lover, and he is so satisfied with himself that he imagines himself in a dream-world as a lord and lover in every respect, with the expectation of even more favours to come.

618 **Lemman, thy grace ... thyn oore** The terminology of courtly love, of the lover pleading for a favour from his adored.

625 **him fil no bet ne wers** Nothing like this had ever happened to him.

632 This is considered by some to be the funniest line in English poetry.

639–40 The description of Absolon trying desperately to cleanse his mouth with anything and everything that comes to hand on the ground is in stark contrast to his earlier toilet preparations.

646 **al yqueynt** Totally extinguished. There is the same association with the noun *queynt* as in line 497.

648 **he sette nat a kers** He didn't give a tinker's cuss.

653 **daun** A corruption of Latin *dominus*, meaning 'master', a title given to persons who hold a university degree. It was also used, as it is here, as a mark of respect. It is the modern equivalent of Mr.

654 **smithed plough harneys** Forged ploughing equipment. There is evidence that blacksmiths worked at night in Chaucer's time.

655 **shaar and kultour** Ploughshare and coulter. These parts are the 'sharp end' of the plough, both being iron blades for cutting and turning the soil.

659 **Cristes sweete tree** The Cross.

662 **upon the viritoot** On the trot. The exact meaning is unknown, but it carries the sense of 'on the move' or 'hopping around'.

663 **Seinte Note** St Neot. A Saxon saint of the ninth century.

664 **Ne roghte nat a bene** Didn't give a damn.

666 **moore tow on his distaf** He had his hands full. Tow is the coarse flax or hemp which was spun into yarn on the distaff. The distaff was a tool for spinning, a sort of rod to which the 'tow' was attached, pulled out into threads and spun on to a reel by hand for subsequent weaving.

672 **nobles alle untold** An uncounted number of gold coins.

674 **Cristes foo** Christ's foe, the devil.

691 **amenden al the jape** Add to the fun.

698 Nicholas's action in all its vulgarity is directly related to Absolon's sensitivity and fastidiousness, and his particular aversion (lines 229–30).

703 **an hande-brede aboute** A piece of skin about the size of a hand shrivelled off.

710 **Nowelis** Noah's, of course. A confusion of 'Noe' and 'Noel' – an understandable mistake by the ignorant carpenter, in his confusion.

713–14 **he foond neither to selle/Ne breed ne ale** He found no time to do business (an expression with the meaning of 'no time for anything'), nor to consider the bread and ale (the provisions for the great escape from the flood). Everything happened so fast that the poor carpenter had no time to consider the situation from the moment he cut the ropes, to crashing on the floor.

718 **bothe smale and grete** Both the humble and those of substance.

722 **stonde he moste unto his owene harm** He stood to fare worse in his injury.

723 **anon bore doun** Immediately interrupted.

726 **Nowelis** See line 710. The corruption is used by Nicholas and Alison to emphasize the confusion and supposed madness of the poor carpenter.

727 **thurgh fantasie** From pure imagining.

731 ***par compaignie***   To keep him company.

746 **God save al the rowte**   God save all the company. This brings
the reader back to the group of pilgrims, and to the link which
introduces the next tale.

Words liable to be mistranslated

The words in the list below closely resemble words used in Modern English, but their meanings are not the same (in some cases quite the opposite), and therefore they must be carefully distinguished from their modern equivalents. Against each word is printed the number of the line in the text where it occurs (or where it first occurs when used a number of times with the same sense), for each word must be considered in its context. Naturally, the Glossary and the Notes should also be consulted.

acquitaunce 219
affeccioun 503
agonie 344
amenden 691
anon, anoon 239, 363, 470
array 339, 522
art 83, 101
avised 476
axe 449
axed 305, 553
been 55, 214
ben 167, 273
bettre 22
bisynesse 535, 546
bord 80, 332
but 59, 187, 188
care 124
chartre 219
clerk 91, 204
compaignie 96, 552
conclusioun 85, 294
confort 573
conseil 395, 422

crouche 371
crul 206
curteisie 15, 179, 243
daun 653
daungerous 230
demen 53, 64, 118
deerne 92, 170, 189
drenche-n 413
faire 181, 214, 460, 591, 635
fame 40
fantasie 83, 727, 732
faste 181, 391, 439, 620
fetisly 97, 211
finding 112
folie 38
froteth 639
game 9, 78, 297
gentil(s) 5, 63, 252
gentillesse 71, 274
greet, grete 70, 718
haliday 201, 232
harlotrie 37
heeld 80, 116

General questions

1 Summarize the plot of *The Miller's Tale*.

2 Discuss the importance of the *Prologue* to the plot and character of *The Miller's Tale*.

3 Absolon has been described as the most interesting character in the *Tale*. Do you agree with this view?

4 Discuss the ways in which Chaucer makes his character descriptions fit the plot of the tale.

5 Trace the development of the different stages of Nicholas's plan, and his deception of the carpenter.

6 What important influence has the medieval tradition of courtly love in *The Miller's Tale*?

7 Consider the part played by either the carpenter or Alison in the *Tale*.

8 It has been said that *The Miller's Tale* is the funniest story in the world. Comment.

9 Discuss the structure of the plot of the *Tale*.

10 Chaucer is a master of comic poetry. Discuss this with reference to *The Miller's Tale*.

11 Chaucer was a great 'painter' with words. Discuss this with reference to *The Miller's Tale*, giving examples from the text.

12 Mathew Arnold commented on Chaucer's liquid music of language. Discuss this with particular reference to Chaucer's versification.

13 We have come to think of Chaucer as a supreme narrative artist. Discuss with reference to the *Tale*.

14 Chaucer was a master of brilliant extended portraiture, where description and character are matched. Discuss with reference to *The Miller's Tale*, and give quotes to illustrate.

15 Chaucer's poetry is full of bright detail. Discuss with reference to *The Miller's Tale*.

16 In *The Miller's Tale*, 'We find ourselves reading a narrative with a modern texture of idiomatic conversation and a well observed detail of daily incident, the whole charged with humour, tenderness and a poetical feeling for actuality.' Discuss.

17 There are no freaks in Chaucer's characters, they are perfectly normal life-size people. Discuss with reference to the *Tale*.

18 From one point of view the story of *The Miller's Tale* is utterly fantastic: from another point of view it is totally realistic. Discuss.

19 Describe the character of Nicholas and the part he plays in the *Tale*.

20 What do we learn about life in Chaucer's time from reading the *Tale*.

21 The host is reluctant to allow the Miller to tell his tale – can you suggest any reason why?

22 On what grounds does Chaucer excuse including *The Miller's Tale* among the others?

23 What evidence is there in the *Tale* that Chaucer was knowledgeable about science?

24 Give a summary of Alison's physical appearance and dress, and suggest how they show her character.

25 Chaucer uses a variety of proverbs or colloquial

expressions in this tale. Quote a few, and explain their meanings.

26 Discuss Absolon's tactics in trying to persuade Alison into granting him her favours.

27 How does a knowledge of grammar help one to enjoy Chaucer's poetry?

28 What evidence is there in this tale that Chaucer was well acquainted with medieval Miracle Plays?

Glossary

Note: Chaucer uses *i* and *y* as equivalents; *ou* and *ow* are interchangeable; as are *-ey-* and *-ay-* (which may also be written *-ei-* or *-ai-*).

The student is advised to consult the Textual notes in association with this Glossary.

abak, aback aback, backwards
abide, abyd abide, wait
abiding awaiting
aboute about, around
accorded agreed
acordaunt in accord, agreeing
acquitaunce legal settlement, deed of release
adoun down, downwards
adrad afraid
affeccioun imagination, fantasy
after after, according to, about
again, ageyn again, in return
agast aghast, terrified
agonie agony, anguish
allone alone
Almageste astronomical treatise
also so, as
alwey always
amenden add to, improve on
amis wrong, wrongly
a-nightes at night
anon, anoon immediately, at once

anonright(es) immediately
ape monkey, fool
apeyren injure, outrage
aright exactly, properly
array array, finery
art university studies (l.83) science (l.101)
aslake assuage, subside
astrelabie astrolabe
astrologie astrology
astromie astronomy
aswowne in a swoon, unconscious
atones at once
atte at, at the
atwinne in twain, in two
atwo in two
augrim stones counters
availleth avails, profits
avalen take off, doff
avised advised, forewarned
aviseth be advised
awook awoke
awroken avenged
ax axe
axe ask, enquire
ay always

ayeyns against, opposite to
baar, beer bore, carried
bad bade, directed
badde bad
balkes beams
barmclooth apron
barred striped, barred
ben to be
bene bean
benedicitee! bless us!
Benedight St Benedict
bent curved, sloped
ber bear oneself, behave
berd beard
berne barn
bet, bettre better
be went is gone
biddeth asks, prays
bifalle, bifel befall, happen
biforn, bifoore before, in
  front
bigan, bigonne began, begun
bigile beguile, deceive
bileve believe, belief or creed
  (l.348)
biseche beseech, beg
biset used
bisily busily, energetically,
  eagerly
bisynesse busyness
bitake commit, entrust,
  deliver
bitide happen
bitwixe between
blake black
blessen bless, refl. cross
  oneself
blew blue

blisful attractive, delightful,
  happy
blosme blossom
bokeler buckler, small shield
bolt bolt, arrow
boos boss
bord board, meals (l.80);
  board, plank (l.332)
boures bower, bed-chamber
bragot bragget, drink made of
  honey and ale
breed bread
brende burned
brest breast, chest
brewhous ale-house
brid bird
brocage mediation, by
  intermediary
brode, brood broad, wide
broghte brought (led, l.568
  Gen. Prol.)
broiden embroidered
brokkinge warbling,
  quavering
brooch brooch
brosten broken
browes eyebrows
bukkes buck's
but but, unless
by cause because
cape gape, stare
care trouble, anxiety
carie carry
carl churl, fellow
cas event, occasion, accident,
  chance
cast device, design
caste(n) throw, cast

Catoun Cato
caughte caught, seized
ceint girdle
celle floor
certein, a a particular number
certein particular
certes certainly
cetewale ginger plant
chambre chamber, room
chartre legal document, deed
chauncel chancel
chaunteth sings
cheere appearance, look
cherl churl, rough fellow
chese choose
chimenee chimney
chippes wood chips
chirche church
cinamome cinnamon
clappe noise, chatter
clapte clapped, shut
clepe call
clerk scholar, student
climben climb
clippe clip (cut hair)
cloisterer monk
clom hush, silence
clomben climbed
clooth cloth, material
cokewold cuckold
cokkes cocks
cole coal
coler collar
com of come on!
compaignie company,
  companions
com pa me come-kiss-me
conclusioun conclusion,
result (of experiment)
confort satisfaction, pleasure
conseil counsel, advice
cop top, (tip)
corde rope
corfew-time curfew time
corn grain
corpus body
cors corpse
corven carved, cut
couched laid, arranged
craft craft, trade, occupation
crepe creep
crie(n) cry, shout
crouche mark with the sign of
  the cross
crul curly
curteisie courtesy, politeness,
  courteous and gentle manners
dar dare
daun master, mister, sir
daunce dance
daungerous disdainful,
  fastidious, affected
debaat conflict, argument
dede, deed dead
deel part, bit, detail
deere dear
deereling darling
deerne secret
defame slander
deffie defy, renounce
degrees ways, manners,
  conditions
deide died
demen deem, judge
  determine
depe deeply, intently

derk dark

desir desire, wish

despeir despair

despit spite, scorn

devel devil

devocioun prayer

deye die

dide put

disporte amuse

distaf distaff, craft tool used for spinning

doke duck

doon(e) do, done

dooth does

dore door

doun down

do wey do away with, take away

drawen draw, retain

drenche(n) drown

dresse direct, go

dressed addressed, positioned, arranged

dreynt drowned

droghte drought, dry weather

dronke(n) drunk

drough, drow drew

dwellen dwell, stay

ech each

echon each one

eek, eke also

eet ate

eft, eftsoones again

eir air

elde age

elles-is else

elves elves, demons

enquere enquire, ask

entente intent, purpose

entred entered, embarked (l.477)

er before

ernest serious intention

ers arse

easily softly, quickly

espie see, discover

estaat state, condition

ete eat

evene even, regular, equal

evere ever, always

everichon each one, everyone

everideel every part, everything

eyen eyes

eyle(th) ail(s)

fair fair, lovely

faire well, properly, suitably, agreeably

falding coarse woollen cloth

falle fallen, happen

falsen falsify, betray

fame renown, (ill) fame (l. 40)

fanne fan

fantasie fancy, interest, (l.83); fantasy, delusion (l.727)

faste fast, quickly, eagerly

fecche fetch, bring

feeldes fields

feeste feast

felaweshipe fellowship, company

fer(re) far

ferde fared (l.349) behaved (l.498)

fetisly handsomely, elegantly, attractively

fey faith
fil fell, happened
filet headband
finding provision, maintenance, support
foison plenty, abundance
folie folly, foolishness
folwinge following
foo foe
foond found
for for, for the sake of, in spite of
forbede forbid
forbere forbear, give way
forheed forehead
forlore lost, ruined
forneys furnace
freendes friends'
frely freely, easily
freres friars
fro from
froteth rubs
ful full, very
furlong way a way apart
gabbe gabble, boast
gailard gay, merry
game game, sport, fun
gan began
gardin-ward towards the garden
gauren gaze, stare
gent slender, graceful
gentil of gentle birth or character
gentillesse courtesy
gentils gentlefolk
gerl girl
gesse guess

gestes guests, lodgers
girdel girdle
giterne cittern, guitar
giterninge guitar playing
gleede coal fire
gnof fellow, lout
goliardeys foul-mouthed buffoon
gon proceed
gonne did
goore gore
goos goose
goost ghost, spirit
gooth goes
grace favour
gracious gracious, attractive
grange granary, barn
graunted granted, accepted
greet, grete great
greyn grain
groneth groans
haaf heaved
haliday holy-day, religious feast day
halves sides, parts
han have
hande-brede hand's breadth
harde hard, tightly
harlotrie wickedness, wicked things, ribaldry
harm harm, injury
harneys equipment, gear
harre hinge, hinges
harrow help! cry of distress
harwed harrowed
haspe hasp, fastening
hastif hasty
hastou hast thou, have you

haunche-bon thigh-bone
heed head, mind (l.420)
heeld held, kept: *heeld to bord*,
  provided board and lodging
  for
heeled healed
heeng, heng hung
heer hair
heere here, hear
heeste behest, command
heeth heather
hem them
hende nice, gentle, polite,
  courteous
hente seize(d)
herbes herbs
herde heard
herestow do you hear?
heris hair(s)
herkneth hearken, listen
Herodes Herod
herte heart
hevene heaven
hevest heave
hewe hue, complexion,
  appearance
hey hay
hidous hideous, terrible
hir, hire her, their
hony honey
hoolinesse saintliness
hoord hoard, store
hooste host, landlord
hoot hot
hors horse
hoses hose, stockings
hou how
houres hours, times

hous house
hust hush, be quiet
hye high
icched itched
ich I
ilke same
imaginacioun imaginings,
  fancy
impressioun effect on the
  mind, obsession
in inn
inquisitif inquisitive, curious
interrogaciouns research,
  experiments
iren iron (instrument)
ivel evil, wrong; ivel biset,
  wronged
janglere noisy fellow, loud
  talker
jalous jealous, suspicious
jape jest, joke, trick, laughing-
  stock
jolif, joly jolly, gay, lively,
  pretty
jubbe jug, vessel for ale
kan know(s)
kembeth, kembd combs,
  combed
keping keeping, caring,
  precautions
kers curse
kiken peep, gaze
kirtel kirtle, tunic
kiste kissed
knarre thick-set fellow
knave boy, servant
kneding trogh kneading
  trough, wooden tub

knokke knock
knowe know, recognize
knowestow do you know?
konne know how to
koude knew how to, knew about
kultour coulter
kymelin wooden tub
labbe blabber-mouth
lasse less
lat let
lat be let be, leave off
laten blood let blood
latoun latten, mixed metal of copper and zinc
laudes lauds, hymns of praise
layen lay
leef leaf, page (l.69), beloved (l.684)
leeste least
leeve dear, beloved
legende life of a saint or martyr
leggen lay
legges legs
leiser leisure, opportunity
lemman lover, sweetheart
lendes loins, thighs
lene lend
lenger longer
lerned learned, studied
lese lose
lether leather
leste pleased
leve see leeve
levere rather
lewed ignorant, unlearned, vulgar, lascivious

leyd laid
licoris liquorice
lief see leeve
light light-hearted, joyous
lightnesse light-heartedness
lik like
likerous lecherous, sexy
lippes lips
list likes, wishes
litel little
lith lie
litherly lazily
lokkes locks of hair
lond land
longinge belonging
loore advice, counsel
looth loathsome, hateful
lorn lost, destroyed
lough laughed
lovely loving, amorous
lyf life, life story
lyk like
maad made
madde become mad
maister master, mister
maistrie mastery, skill
make game play
maken make
maladie sickness
male bag, parcel
man one, anyone
maner-e manner, way, sort
marle-pit clay pit
mateere subject matter
m'athinketh it seems to me
may can
meede bribe, a gift of money
meenes intermediaries

meeth mead, a drink made from honey

meke meek, gentle

melodie melody, music

men people, folk

merveille wonder

mete meat, food

mette dreamed

mighte could

mightily mightily, powerfully

mirie merry

mirthe mirth, enjoyment

mislay lay awkwardly

misse miss, fail

misspeke speak incorrectly, mispronounce

mo more

mooder mother

moorne mourn, yearn

moot may, must

moralitee morality, moral writing

morne morning

morwe (to)morrow

moste must

mous mouse

mowe may

nam am not

namely particularly, specially

namoore no more

narwe closely, tightly

nas was not

nat not

natheless nonetheless

ne nor, not

nede need, requirement

nedeth, needeth needs, is necessary

nether lower

newe new, lately, recently

nie nigh, close, near at hand

night-spel prayer against spirits

nis is not

niste did not know

noble gold coin

Noe Noah

noght nought, nothing, not at all

nolde would not

nones nonce, occasion

noon none, not any

noot don't know

noote tune, song

nosethirles nostrils

Note St Neot

Nowelis Noel's

offringe offering, collection

o, oon one

oold old

oore gracious favour

ooth, othes oath(s)

ordinance command, decree

Osenay, Oseneye Oseney

owene own

Oxenford Oxford

paas, pas pace

paramours lovers

pardee by God

parfay by my faith

passioun passion, agony

pater-noster Pater-noster, prayer, Lord's prayer

pere-jonette early pear

perled pearled, beaded

Petres Peter's

pich pitch
piggesnie a little flower, sweetheart, darling
piment spiced and sweetened wine
pley(e) play, amuse
plogh plough
point-devis neatly, fastidiously
pointes laces, lacings finished with tags at the ends
poke bag, pouch
popelote doll, darling, pet
Poules St Paul's
poure poor
preche preach
presse cupboard
preye pray, ask
preyere prayer
prime prime, the period between six to nine in the morning
primerole primrose, darling, pet
privee secret, discreet
prively secretly
privetee secrecy, secret purpose or affairs
profred proffered
propre fine, splendid
proprely properly, handsomely
protestacioun public announcement
prye pry, peer
purs purse
purveiaunce preparations
putteth thrusts

quake quake, tremble
queynte strange, curious, artful, sly, graceful
quinible high-pitched voice, treble voice
quite requite, match
quod said
rage behave with abandon
ram prize for wrestling
rated berated, rebuked
rathe early
raughte reached
rede, reed red
redy ready
reed advice
reherce repeat, recount
rekene recount, tell
remedie remedy
remenant rest, remainder
renning running
rente (private) income
reson explanation
revel revelry
rewe have pity
reweth grieves, distresses
richesse riches, wealth
right truly, exactly
ris branch, spray
rist rose
rode complexion
roghte cared
rometh wanders, goes
rong rang
ronges rungs
ronnen ran
route, rowte company, group
rubible lute, fiddle
rude rough, ignorant, vulgar

Sathanas Satan
saugh saw
sautrie psaltery
savourly appetizingly, with relish
scaffold scaffold, stage on wheels
scole school
scoler scholar
Salomon Solomon
see sea
seide(e) said
seil sail
seistow say you
sely happy, blessed; wretched, unlucky; good, kind
sencer censer
sensinge censing
seyn, seye say, tell, mean
shaar ploughshare
shal should
shaltow shall you
shapen devise, plan, plot
sharpeth sharpens
shette shut
shilde forbid
shippes bord aboard ship
shode hair parting
sholde should
sholdres shoulders
shoon shone
shoos shoes
shour(es) shower, rain, rainfall
shot-windowe casement window
sik sigh, groan
sikerly, sikirly surely, certainly
siketh sighs
similitude likeness
sin, sith since
sinne sin
sit sat
sitten sit
sleigh, slie sly, crafty, subtle
slomber slumber, sleep
sloo sloe-berry
smal(e) small, neat, slender, humble
smert pain
smithed forged
smok smock
smoot smote, struck
snare snare, trap
sodeinly suddenly
softe softly, quickly
solas delight, amusement, pleasure
som, somme some
somdeel somewhat
somwhat something
sond sand
song sang, singing
sonne sun
soun sound
soore sorely, pitifully
sooth true, truth
soothly truly
sorwe sorrow, grief
sory sad, sorrowful
soster sister
sowis eris sow's ear(s)
space space, time
spak spoke
speche speech, talk

spedde Sped, hurried
speed(e) speed, hurry
spek(e) speak
spie spy, look at
spille perish, die
spitously sharply, unkindly
spouse husband
springe spring up, down
sproong sprang, jumped up
squaymous squeamish
staf staff, pole
stalkes uprights
stalketh stalks, goes stealthily
stant stands
stele steel, steal
sterres stars
sterte, stirte started, leapt
stille still, quickly, motionless
stint stop
stiringe moving
ston, stoon stone
stonde onto submit to, accept
stondeth stands
storial history, describing events
streight straight
strete street
strokes striking, rough treatment
strook blow
strouted sprouted, jutted
stryf conflict
studiyng studying, studiousness
sturdily sturdily, strongly
subtile subtle, artful
suffisant sufficient
suffiseth suffices, satisfies

suite matching type
surplis surplice
swalwe swallow
sweete sweetly
swelte swelter
swerd sword
swere swear
swete sweat
swich such
swimme float
swinke(n) toil, work
swived possessed, enjoyed, laid (sexually)
swogh sigh, groan
swoor swore, exclaimed
swoote sweet
tapes tapes, ribbons
tappestere tapster
tarie tarry, wait
tasseled tasselled
teche teach
tete teat
thakked stroked, patted
thanne thin
that who
thenche think, imagine
thenk think
ther where
thikke thickly, plentifully
thilke this, that
thinketh it seems
thise these
tho those, then
thoghte thought, intended
thombe thumb
thonder-dent thunder-clap
thoughte seemed
thre three

thresshfold threshold

thriftily properly, carefully, in a workmanlike way

thrive thrive, prosper

throte throat, voice

tikel uncertain

til till to

tolden told

tollen thries three times (his proper) toll

tonge tongue

toucheth touches (on)

toun town, parish

Tour Tower of London

toute, towte backside, bum

tow tow, coarse part of flax or hemp

travaille travail, suffering

trave frame for holding horses

trewe true, honest, faithful

trewely truly

trewe-love charm

trippe trip, dance

trouthe word of honour

trowe believe

tubbe tub

turtel turtle-dove

tweye two

unbokeled unbuckled, unfastened, opened

underspore thrust under (to force upwards)

undertake undertake, guarantee

unnethe uneasily, hardly, scarcely with difficulty

until to

unto into

untold uncounted

upright upright, upwards

vanitee foolishness

vengeaunce vengeance

verraily truly

verray true

verye note l.377

viritoot note l.662

vitaille victuals, food

vitailled victualled, provisioned

vois voice

voluper headdress, cap

wafres wafer-cakes

waget light blue

waille wail, cry

waite await

wake keep awake, stay up

wal wall

walwinge wallowing, rolling in

wan pale

war aware

warante warrant, undertake

wasshen washed

wedde-n wed, marry

weel well

weileth wails

wel well, much, fully (used emphatically)

wenche wenche, maidservant

wende supposed, believed

wentestow did you go?

werede wore

werk work

werken work, act, make

werkes works, acts, deeds

wers-e worse

werte wart
wery weary
wether(es) ram
wey way
weylawey alas!
wezele weasel
which what
whilom once (upon a time)
whit white
wight person
wightes creatures, spirits
wilde wild
wile crafty trick
wille will
winsinge restless, impatient
wirche work
wiste knew
wit wit, mind, reason;
  intelligence, understanding
wite know
wo woe
wol will, wish, want
wolle wool
wonnen won
wont is wont, accustomed
wood mad, insane
woostou do you know?
woot know, knows
wordes words
woweth woos
wreye betray
wrightes workman,
  tradesman
wrooth wrathful, enraged
wryed twisted, turned
wyf wife

yaf gave
ybete beaten
yblent blinded
ybleynt started back, turned
  aside
yboght brought
yborn carried
yclad clad, dressed
ycleped called
ycovered covered
ycrowe crowed
ydight decorated
ye you, eye
yeer year
yeman yeoman
yerne eager, lively, quick
yeve give
yfalle fallen
yforged forged, minted
yfounde found
ygeten got
ygrave engraved
yheere hear
yherd haired, covered with
  hair
yleid laid
ynogh, ynowe enough
yong young
yoore yore, of old, long ago
ypulled pulled, plucked
yqueynt quenched,
  extinguished
ysworn sworn
ytake taken
ytoold told
ywis certainly